REMAIN IN ME

REMAIN IN ME

Holy Orders, Prayer, and Ministry

JAMES KEATING

Paulist Press
New York / Mahwah, NJ

Cover image copyright © by Servizio Fotografico--L'Osservatore Romano
Cover design by Tamian Wood
Book design by Lynn Else

Library of Congress Cataloging-in-Publication Data
Names: Keating, James, author.
Title: Remain in me : holy orders, prayer, and ministry / James Keating.
Description: New York : Paulist Press, [2019] | Includes bibliographical references.
Identifiers: LCCN 2018029767 (print) | LCCN 2018042204 (ebook) | ISBN 9781587687921 (e-book) | ISBN 9780809154159 (pbk. : alk. paper)
Subjects: LCSH: Catholic Church—Clergy—Religious life. | Spiritual direction—Catholic Church.
Classification: LCC BX1912.5 (ebook) | LCC BX1912.5 .K435 2019 (print) | DDC 248.8/92—dc23
LC record available at https://lccn.loc.gov/2018029767

ISBN 978-0-8091-5415-9 (paperback)
ISBN 978-1-58768-792-1 (e-book)

Published by Paulist Press
997 Macarthur Boulevard
Mahwah, New Jersey 07430

www.paulistpress.com

Printed and bound in the
United States of America

Dedicated to
Kathy Kanavy, MA
Trudy McCaffrey

Gifted spiritual directors to the clergy

In gratitude to
Fr. Peter Ryan SJ, STD
Msgr. Gerard McCarren, STD

Gifted theologians in service to clergy
formation and spiritual direction

CONTENTS

FOREWORD

James Keating, the dynamic spiritual theologian at the Institute for Priestly Formation at Creighton University, offers here a wonderful, essential reflection on spirituality for priests and deacons. One might express first the strong hope that this book will be read extensively by priests and those studying for the priesthood, and, of course, by deacons as well. The fact that the author is a permanent deacon in the Church would seem to require this insistence on the book's importance for priests and seminarians. In general, priests, unless truly humble, are not inclined to take instruction from the services of a deacon. The prejudgment in this case will be to their loss and detriment. The insights presented here on priestly spiritual life are serious and simply nonnegotiable. Every deacon reading the work will likewise gain spiritually. The reflections clearly derive from long spiritual commitment, wide reading, and much prayer, experience, and reflection.

The cornerstone animating the work is the crucial importance of prayer. Deacon Keating does more than propose the rejuvenation of a perennial need for committed prayer in clerical life. His experience as spiritual director has informed him with a sensitivity for the obstacles that so often intrude on the clerical life and lead to a slow drifting away from a foundational need. The supernatural battle at work in the life of prayer, for instance, is quite starkly exposed. As Deacon Keating writes, "Satan hates clerics who pray." Even more, therefore, do we need to maintain daily hunger for time in the presence of a tabernacle for any real fruitfulness in clerical life. The subtle ease with which exterior busyness can occupy a cleric's day, replacing the need for prayer, is often excused and rationalized. The result is the empty soul unable to bring Christ to others. There are wonderful passages and striking quotations that animate the reader's hunger to return to the daily practice of sacred time before the Lord in solitude and silence.

An interesting observation is the importance of spiritual direction if one is to continue the pursuit of prayer in a serious manner. The obstacles encountered in the daily practice of silent prayer are numerous and often unanticipated. It is easy to become confused, discouraged, and to curtail the daily commitment. In Deacon Keating's view, the steadiness of a commitment to prayer is often aligned to a readiness to remain committed to spiritual direction. Deacon Keating offers keen insights on the value of spiritual direction as an opportunity to explore deeply into the mysterious conversation of God with the soul as it confronts the divine presence at work in a way that is not always so clear and manageable. As he says so well, "We don't need a spiritual director because prayer is complex; we need a director because we are complex."

The book strongly reaffirms the Christlike identity inherent in clerical life. The work of the priest and deacon is a labor for souls in union with Christ's love for souls. *Remain in Me* makes clear that a rootedness in the Mass and the mystery of the renewed sacrifice present there is at the heart of such lives. The life of the priest and deacon is to flow out of a receptive interiority that is cultivated in union with Christ himself. The pursuit of serious interiority is a great challenge today, and great because our own contemporary time pushes us constantly to exterior focus and the scattering of our energies and concentration. Deacon Keating is among those who propose a recovery of the contemplative dimension of life reinserted into the work we are given to do for the Church and for souls. A contemplative relationship with Christ—deep, committed, and daily practiced—brings a different quality of soul into all encounters of a day. This contemplative component is arguably the primary need for every priest and deacon to recognize in his vocation. *Remain in Me* gives us precisely a rich resource for awakening that contemplative desire among priests and deacons. If with the help of grace, this book succeeds in that mission, it will do a great service in the contemporary Church. Let us hope these reflections find a generous and receptive response from many priests, seminarians, and deacons.

Fr. Donald Haggerty, STD
St. Patrick's Cathedral
New York, New York

INTRODUCTION

*The [Second Vatican] Council called [priests]
instructors in the faith; there is no better way to be
such instructors than by devoting your best efforts
to the growth of your communities in the faith....The
deacons...who you have the good fortune to have with
you are your natural assistants in [these efforts].*

—John Paul II, *Catechesi Tradendae*,
October 16, 1979 (no. 64)

Over the last few decades, the collaboration of priests and deacons
in the ministry of the gospel has not been without some emotional
tension. As we celebrate the fiftieth anniversary of the restoration of
the permanent diaconate in the Catholic Church, we enter a new
day in the vital relationship between these two grades of holy orders.
This new day welcomes a cooperative, creative, and prayer-imbued
communion between priests and deacons who labor as one to serve the
spiritual needs of parishioners. This book promotes such a communion
by addressing the interior lives of priests and deacons simultaneously.
The sacrament of holy orders is itself the very gift that binds priests and
deacons as "natural" allies in the work of the gospel.

I encourage parish priests and deacons to study this book prayerfully together, perhaps using it as common spiritual reading. Once
read, these same priests and deacons will find that conversing together
about its contents may yield a new resolve for a cooperative mission.
Furthermore, mindful of these conversational graces, I invite clergy to
use this book as a springboard for mutual spiritual conversation and
pastoral planning. In such conversations, the "natural" union between

priests and deacons becomes clearer and carries the potential to ignite a brotherhood of creative pastoral thinking, better serving the mission of the parish.

The book is not directed to providing practical ways of deepening the unity between the two orders, but rather, it addresses their mutual dedication to remain with Christ in prayer, even while serving parishioners. Once prayer becomes habituated in the heart, compassion grows for those who look for God "like sheep without a shepherd." Through interior prayerfulness, clerical unity in ministry can be better insured. Holy orders fastens a man's heart to Christ, who reveals that his own heart is fastened upon the lost sheep. Paying heed to Christ's deepest desire "that my house may be filled" (Luke 14:23), the unity of priests and deacons can only benefit those who desire to come into that house.

As you read this book, you will notice some repetition of themes. This is intentional. It is my hope that priests and deacons will use this book in their prayer time, on retreat, or during the holy seasons of Lent and Advent. Encountering such thematic repetition allows the truths they bear to water the imagination like waves coming ashore and receding, or recurrent verses in poetry.

The great struggle of the spiritual life is to find ways to stay in love with God. May the following meditations encourage priests and deacons to believe that such struggle is well worth it, especially as it mysteriously bears fruit in the lives of the people Christ has asked us to serve.

I

SPIRITUAL DIRECTION

To live a life of loving communion with the Holy Spirit is one of the most courageous, emotional, and moral commitments we can live. This life of communion, by its own nature, demands courage because the One with whom we are fascinated cannot be seen or heard or touched, nor does he guarantee continuing streams of interior affective consolation. Men think that climbing mountains without ropes is courageous, and it is, but nothing surpasses the courage of a cleric who commits his life to noticing the movements of divine love within his own heart, receiving that love, and then sharing the fruit of such love with the people he serves in ministry.

In the spiritual life, courage is needed because doubt and fear arise. Such doubt and fear can appear within our hearts if we fail to detect affectively the presence of the Spirit in our prayer and ministry. When God appears to slip from the grasp of our emotional life, we may drift from daily prayer—no longer defining our daily lives by our relationship with God but only by the press of tangible commitments flooding our day. To remain with the Spirit in prayer over decades, knowing affective consolation or its absence is indeed an expression of fortitude.

To drift from a habit of prayer is a sad surprise within our busy ministry. We can recede from prayer and from receiving the love of God so subtly that, before we become fully aware of what we are choosing, our prayer lives have diminished. As clerics, we are busy in two ways: (1) in responding to the spiritual needs of people, and (2), in managing the burden of our own constitution, wounds, neuroses, and sin. As the needs of others shower us or as we notice the weight of our

1

own emotional or spiritual suffering, we can miss the Spirit loving us. Now, of course, there are integrated times in our lives as well; times when we receive deep love from God and when we remain emotionally and spiritually available to our people's needs. Such integration is established when our capacity to suffer the coming of God's love is welcomed. I say "suffer" God's love because his offer to enter our lives with divine life is often resisted because we prefer the status quo. God is always doing something *new*. However, God introducing new things into our "routine" may seem more a threat than a promise. So, we resist. We also resist God's love because we prefer the immediate gratification of our false gods to the more deliberate and developing communion with him that does not quickly assuage our struggles. God's love is communion; it is not a "quick fix." His love is purification, not affirmation of our status quo; it is elevation and "newness" rather than an extension of our own will. So, *to suffer the love* of God is, in fact, the condition of our fallen humanity. We should *desire* to be loved by God, but, instead, we hide from his love (see Gen 3:9).

As the saints testify, we can gradually become spiritually integrated if we remain committed to prayer and vulnerable to the truth God communicates about himself and ourselves. The saints give us an example of how we suffer this integration and attain spiritual health. Theirs is the way of robust engagement with the eucharistic mystery, the sacrament of reconciliation, therapeutic counseling, love of family and friends, attentiveness to those in need, and for some, even physical suffering in union with Calvary. All these sources, in which the saint participates, brings them emotional integration, peace, and wisdom, but engaging in any or all of these things alone, without the benefit of a spiritual director, may risk the loss of grace to our fleeting memories and busy calendars. The golden thread of spiritual maturity is spiritual direction. Our lives as clerics are not ones of choosing between spiritual direction *or* the Mass; spiritual direction *or* therapy (if needed); prayer *or* ministry. Instead, our clerical lives involve the joyously Catholic integration of all these elements (and more) simultaneously. We clerics have a feast of resources to mend our hearts and secure our presence to people in need. One of our greatest expressions of love for the Church is to undergo our own needed healing and ongoing formation. Before exploring the topics of healing and spiritual direction, we must reflect on the nature of our interior life itself. This will prepare us for a richer discussion on spiritual direction later.

VULNERABLE TO LOVE

As humans, one of our perennial weaknesses is a fickle stance toward life in the Spirit. We want to pray but we are often inexplicably drawn to the tasks at hand, leaving prayerful desire to die at its first prompting. One truth that helps us stay committed to a spiritual life is knowledge that such a life is not another task to be accomplished. Entering prayer has less to do with task completion and more to do with receiving gifts. At its core, the spiritual life is about "receiving more" rather than "doing more." Prayer is not my work; it is God's healing. In noting that receptivity is at the core of prayer, we have just uncovered the root logic of 1 Thessalonians 5:17 when it counsels us to pray always. As our interior lives become attuned to receiving love from God, we realize such can become a continuing disposition. We can *become* men *who are vulnerable* to being loved by God:

> There is nothing more to do than to let [the will of God] act and abandon ourselves to it, blindly with perfect confidence.…There is the drachma of the Gospel, the treasure which we do not find because we suppose it to be too far away. Do not ask me what the secret is for finding this treasure. There is no secret. The treasure is everywhere. It is offered to us at all times, in all places.…Let us open our mouths, and they shall be filled. Divine action inundates the universe.…We have nothing to do but be carried by its waves.[1]

The Holy Spirit counters our false notion that the spiritual life is our task alone by actively moving toward us to give himself away through prayer. It takes courage to sustain a fascination with the Holy Spirit, especially when the senses lay fallow in such, but the Spirit is eager to initiate and sustain communion with us. Even if the Spirit is beyond our senses,[2] he is not inert in this relationship but *actively* in love. He presses toward us from within to affect a true communion known in faith, but we must be vulnerable to this "press" toward our hearts and receive love as the foundation of our very identity. In other words, our identity is not secured, discovered, or guaranteed by accomplishment, but by making ourselves prayerfully available to divine life communicated sacramentally and personally. Interior availability in

3

faith is the foundation on which one builds a spiritual life unto death. Noticing the affective movements of our heart in its thoughts, feelings, and desires keeps us at the portal of God's arrival. He comes to give himself from within these interior movements, movements that carry truth, itself, and us into truth. To name our thoughts, feelings, and desires before God is to secure our lives in truth. Just as it is "work" for a married couple to stay in love, so it is in the spiritual life. But this "work" is a paradoxical effort of being vulnerable, available, and open to *receive* love. The spiritual life is not an effort to attract love. Astoundingly, we are already attractive to God. Even more mysteriously, like a physician to pain, Christ is attracted to our sin. Hence, one of our greatest temptations—to purify ourselves unto divine approval—is wasted energy. No physician demands we be healed before he attends to our wounds. So it is with Christ. Somehow, he is attracted to a beauty in our wounds (see Luke 10:34). Our accepting such a truth about our vulnerability is a key decision in the drama of sustaining and deepening our communion with God.

Some men think that "talk about receptivity" is weak and, disparagingly, feminine. Such a biased and defensive reaction needs to be addressed clearly as nonsense. To receive is not feminine; *it is human.* For some reason, women are generally more adept at emotional vulnerability, listening, and suffering in the service of communion with others. That is their glory. Their clear headedness about these virtues does not mean that men need to be muddled about them to be masculine. Human love involves both self-donation and reception of the other. The clearest expression where *receptivity* and *giving* establish a person as human is the marital act itself. The moral theologian William May said it best when describing the marital act as one wherein "a woman receives in a giving sort of way, and a man gives in a receiving sort of way."[3] One cannot give without receiving; one cannot receive without giving. To do so would be the subversion of love. Of course, one can refuse to give or refuse to receive, but those dispositions are the very spiritual pathologies that harm progress in our sustained communion with God.

Such a resistance to the full ebb and flow of love ought not to be present in a spiritual person. True conversion reaches its apex when moral and spiritual freedom inhabit a person who offers no resistance to the ebb and flow of love. This freedom can be described as "the burden of achieving giving way to the surprise of receiving."[4]

LOVE AS SUFFERING

For clerics, in their call to be configured to Christ, this expression of achievement giving way to receiving can be the very mark of our masculine lives. The burden of accomplishment, giving, and task is the burden of the cross: "It is finished" (John 19:30). It is, however, not simply the cross of giving. Love is always reciprocity. Even within the cross, within such depletion of self in giving, is the surprise that *within itself* is the anticipation of what will be received. Deep within the crucifixion, within its self-donation, is the *gift* of resurrection from the Father as response. All love is giving and receiving. When one gives to another, an emotional wound, a vulnerability, is incurred. Such an act opens the giver to receive love from the other. The mystery of love on earth is simply one of cruciformed receptivity:[5] a giving in the service of love, and a receiving of love because of such giving.

It is true that, as clerics, we might envision our spiritual lives to be "our" accomplishment or failure. In the end, the spiritual life is not a personal accomplishment or failure; it is, instead, an awakening to the presence of God as love at the very core of our being. God's loving presence is faithfully turned toward us, a presence eager to accompany and initiate communion and looking only for a response to its own beauty. This may sound like cheap grace, but spiritual living is *only* our response to beauty. In the context of knowing this beauty, Divine Beauty, what it elicits is costly indeed (see Luke 19:1–10 for what beauty elicits, and Mark 10:22 for what even beauty cannot reach). Knowing such beauty calls forth self-gift, which can be an excruciating relinquishment of our natural self-involvement. We call this self-gift the moral life, a calling forth of love to be enacted in our fallen world, where the choice to love involves a suffering:

> Anyone who really wanted to get rid of suffering would have to get rid of love before anything else, because there can be no love without suffering, because it always demands an element of self-sacrifice…it will always bring with it renunciation and pain. When we know that the way of love—this exodus, this going out of oneself—is the true way by which man becomes human, then we also understand that suffering is the process through which we mature.…Love itself

is a passion, something we endure. In love…I am taken out of my comfortable tranquility and have to let myself be reshaped. If we say that suffering is the inner side of love, we then also understand it is so important to learn how to suffer—and why, conversely, the avoidance of suffering renders someone unfit to cope with life. He would be left with an existential emptiness, which could then only be combined with bitterness, with rejection and no longer with any inner acceptance or progress toward maturity.[6]

To allow oneself to be loved, the future pope is saying, is to allow oneself to be "found." Love is suffering because it draws out of us our true condition, a condition we have been hiding from others. The one who loves us is like a searching light in his or her fascination with us. Love wants to know; love wants to revel in our real presence. The suffering that is love is the pain that is known when sinners attempt to reveal themselves after a lifetime of emotional reserve, independent living, and self-concern. Love's suffering is the pain of coming to life as a gift for another. Ultimately, being such a gift and remaining in a posture of self-giving will become joy, not pain. In the beginning of love, however, the process of "letting myself be reshaped" by the beloved is a curious burden that I do not want to put down.

To say that there is suffering in love is not to say that love is depressing or that it carries only heaviness. In fact, love is the pervasion of happiness in a person. Before this happy reality inhabits a person's heart, however, love first begins as an invitation to turn from the distraction of idols (immediate gratification) and instead to choose vulnerability before the Divine Beauty. Divine Beauty is the ministry and person of Christ and to contemplate it gives imagination a new weight and substance.[7] Such a transition in interests can take time, patience, and a practice of hope as we await a new substantial communion with God. Hope is needed as we place our trust in the promise of God's love, even as our imaginations may be tempted to return to our former ways of seeking artificial consolation in our sins and idolatries. We may want God to fill the space vacated by these idols of "immediacy" instantaneously; however, because the decision to worship idols is real, we first need to be purified of these past choices. Then, we need to be empowered by grace to become *attracted to the good* and beautiful, as our vices linger in the memory ready to call us back to their recent and attractive ways of supplying immediate satisfaction. Just as St. Augustine's repudiated sins cried out to him, "Do you think you can live without us?"[8]

To say that love is suffering is to say that one *must undergo* love in some sense; one must burn "passively" in the presence of Divine Beauty and receive it as real, even if we do not feel we deserve to be in his presence. This passive side of love puts to rest the myth that love is owed to me because of some trait I possess. Love is never owed; it is always endured, received, and responded to in gratitude and worship: "I adore *you!*"

Love looks to the other. Our natural state is to look to our own satisfaction, and so love takes the form of the cross, of sacrifice. To connect with God in the Spirit, we are invited to behold God in the flesh—Jesus Christ. Thank God he came in the flesh! Because he came among us, we now have what we crave as men: actions to behold and contemplate, virtues displayed to inspire and enact. Since Pentecost, and our own baptisms, we have even more: divine power from within! Even as his presence and power dwell within us, we are called to contemplate the historical life of Christ and welcome the actions of Christ into our imagination, into a new way of thinking.

By beholding the life, death, and resurrection of Christ in prayer and *lectio divina*—and by participating in this mystery in the eucharistic liturgy—we can discern all things with a new imagination. This imagination is sacred, born of faith and surrender to Christ. Each vocation specifies this imagination, and, through it, Christ reaches our minds to facilitate our living them more fully. Specifically, Christ influences our minds as priests and deacons with his own sacrificial and servant mysteries (See John 13:14–15; 15:18–27; Luke 22:27). The experience of being moved by these mysteries opens us to live out of an authentic clerical imagination. Only when one has experienced these mysteries as real does the mind conspire with the affect to secure a new fount of imagery. From this fount flows our thoughts, prayers, and ministries. This new imagination diminishes our interest in the distractions of this passing age (Rom 12:1–2) and fixes our attention on our ministries out of love for Christ.[9]

This love leads us to contemplate the suffering Christ, which, over time and in the Spirit, heals our wounded reason (CCC §2037). Such contemplation allows the truth of the scriptural texts to enter the conscience and the heart and to order them toward communion with

God and, therefore, conversion of life. Such is the nature of true theological thinking; it is healed thinking. Healed thinking is born because
of explicit and sustained contemplation of the mysteries of Christ in
faith; mysteries that are not exhausted in past events in Jerusalem but
carry encounters with the living Christ within the Church, its sacramental life, and our personal prayer lives as clergy. This is the "suffering" that we are called to assume: to open our minds to the living
influence of the paschal mystery of Christ, sacramentally participate
in this mystery, and establish our comprehension upon Christ doing
"his thinking within us."[10] Christ "thinking within" us is not a mystical exceptionalism; it is born from intentionally relating our minds to
Christ's in prayer. In this, our minds are formed anew, and revelation
is understood in love, taking us beyond the minds we once had to a
new way of conceiving reality in and through the mystery of Christ.
Clergy, then, are invited to be leaders in suffering the coming of Christ
by becoming affectively and intellectually vulnerable to his truth and
beauty. Such vulnerability indicates an eagerness to have intimacy
with the Trinity and to live within that intimacy as our vocation.

THE HEALING GAZE OF LOVE

The more we gaze upon a crucifix in prayer, regularly enter *lectio
divina*, or ponder the needs of the poor in the presence of the Blessed
Sacrament, the grip this "current age" has on our imagination slack-
ens, and we are gifted with a new mind. Speaking about the biblical
story of the prodigal son, J. Brian Bransfield notes,

> From the moment we go off track, God the Father gazes
> into the distance between us and him. It is his look, his
> grace, even when we are in sin, that wakes us up again and
> inspires in us the desire and longing for repentance. This
> is known as prevenient grace, a grace that comes to us to
> encourage us to turn back to God.[11]

God is always gazing at us hoping to awaken us to a new way of
thinking and acting. The imagination is powerful in its capacity to take
us more deeply into reality, especially when images relate to and define

one another. One example is when we pray with the crucifix and then see the sacrifices that other clergy make in service of the Church all around us. The Bridegroom's life from the cross is recognized in such relentless self-giving by the clergy, and we are inspired to go deeper into that self-gift ourselves. The imagination is powerful in another way as well; in its capacity to denigrate a man's character. In this case, only the purifying images of Christ's mysteries loosen the grip that the culture of distraction has on our minds. Gazing in adoration upon the Blessed Sacrament or opening our hearts within *lectio divina* will, over time and in the presence of a sound mind, recover one's grasp of reality and birth within us a spiritual and creative ministry. Being lost in the wasteland of popular culture compounds our native self-involvement, pulling us further from creativity and hastening a plummet into self-centered darkness. This darkness cannot be the origin of ministry and so there is an urgency felt by the Church to liberate clergy from imprisonment in the self.

Becoming aware each day of what one thinks about, imagines, and desires—be it inspired or degrading—is part of the prerequisite work of entering spiritual direction. Long before we even find a spiritual director after ordination, we are invited to enter the presence of the Holy Trinity each day and withstand the pain of self-examination. In this way, we become aware of our own interiority in the emotional safety of prayer. One can confidently say that prayer is the safest emotional place on earth.[12] In prayer, when the image of God held in the heart is genuine, we can receive truths about ourselves while simultaneously welcoming Divine Love. Here is the integration that moves us to healing and spiritual maturation. This self-knowledge is, however, only as real as one's engagement with the Trinity in loving prayer. Our identity is *bestowed* and secured by God; it is not achieved or *won* by will. In Christ, through the sacramental life, we are all beloved sons in whom the Father is well pleased (see Matt 3:17). What is happening at the deepest level of being, our existence as beloved, can be contemplated in grace-filled prayer and within the imagination born of the biblical revelation of Christ. Who we are can be known and secured as we share with God all that we are noticing interiorly. As our prayer life deepens, we become more conscious that our whole life is being given from God. From this consciousness, we are awakened, and our desire to worship—*to give thanks*[13]—is enflamed. As we move to a life of worship, we again receive God, and our true self is safeguarded in such

9

a life. At Mass, we consciously offer ourselves into the self-offering of Christ to the Father in the Spirit as our way of *salvation*. This salvation is now our deepest identity; men who come to be healed of all wounds and integrated into the Source of our own being.

Certainly, all of these foundational truths about our being in Christ influence our prayer at some level but are never fully held in consciousness during every prayer. In fact, much of prayer is simply enduring an almost predictable silence. This silence can appear to be "empty" and without love, even as faith tells us such silence is "full" and carries with it an irrevocable promise: God is with us "in the name of the Father, Son, and Holy Spirit." Unfortunately, this experience of prayer as empty, even as we know that somehow Christ is active *in* this prayerful emptiness, is one of the common reasons that clergy stop praying.

During times of emptiness, routine, and duty in prayer, it is our spiritual director who may be carrying just the grace we need to "show up" again before the Blessed Sacrament or the crucifix or open the Bible and "burn" with patience as we await the coming of God. The work of staying in love with God is about remaining steady and committed to prayer, even if such prayer is one long exercise in suffering the absence of consoling affective movements. Pope Benedict XVI spoke of this kind of prayer as a "struggle…a long night of seeking God's face" so he will bless us. This blessing that we seek, however, cannot be "grabbed or won through our own strength but must be received as gift."[14]

SPIRITUAL DIRECTION AS GIFT[15]

One gift that we can receive is wisdom from our spiritual director about such struggles in prayer. It is, however, no secret that good spiritual directors are difficult to find. There was a day when many in the Church thought that the best directors could only be monks, or friars, or nuns; those who spent the bulk of their day in prayer. Diocesan priests, not to mention deacons, were regarded as too busy with sacramental ministry and the administration of parishes, and thus unable to "seek his Face" in prayer. Such a stereotype carried some truth, as diocesan priests do not pray exactly as religious do. But how they pray is still prayer! We have found in our own day that not only do diocesan clergy pray, but they can, with proper training and steady prayer, be excellent spiritual directors.

Whether we choose a religious, diocesan clergy, or layperson for our director, we are looking for a few things: first and foremost, someone who prays. This may seem obvious, but we shouldn't take the advice of the saints too literally when they counsel to choose an intelligent person rather than a pious person for a spiritual director (St. Teresa of Avila). The two are not mutually exclusive if we understand the word *pious* to mean "simply prayerful," rather than in a pejorative way. In fact, one who prays engages in an activity that enlightens the mind. We can't necessarily say one's IQ goes up when one has a habit of prayer, but we can say that one who prays is imbued with a wisdom born of a relationship with the divine. Second, it certainly helps if one's director is intelligent in the ways of theology, and in the practice and training of spiritual direction. Third, I would also suggest that the spiritual director should be nonideological. A director is positioned to listen to our interior lives, not to promote a psychological, political, or devotional agenda. He or she is one who listens with a *sacramental and doctrinal mind and heart*. Finding such a person can be a challenge, but such people do exist and are, even now, laboring in the Church with the "mind of Christ." Such a mind is attained through a study and love of the saints, doctrine, worship, and the moral and anthropological truths housed within Catholicism.

SPIRITUAL DIRECTION AS PRAYER

Primarily, spiritual direction should itself be an experience of prayer. The role of the director is to create an environment wherein we can better listen to God within our own heart and mind. The director establishes himself or herself as one who carries a simple question: "What has Christ been doing in your prayer lately?" As we begin to share this activity, which will always be an account of God giving himself to us in some fashion,[16] we realize that this gift of spiritual direction allows us to recall, or better, experience afresh, how God has been loving us. The prerequisite for any fruitful spiritual direction session is noticing God acting in the ordinariness of our days, and in our interior affective movements (e.g., I feel alone, loved, peaceful, and so on). It is spiritual direction that invites us to be vulnerable to divine love as God wills to express it.

Prayer, then, is God reaching us with his love. As Benedict XVI noted, "Prayer is pure receptivity."[17] God's perennial stance toward us is self-giving love. What makes prayer a chore, at times, is that we can "harden" ourselves against God's outpouring of love. To pass through periods of such hardening is an experience of knowing what it means to need a savior. This hardening devolves into all sorts of self-imposed sufferings, which may layer our days in darkness instead of light, imagination, and joy. Spiritual directors notice such stances within us and suggest ways to return to light. They do this primarily through one invitation: Remain in Jesus, remain available to him, and be open to his initiatives of love. This is a difficult invitation because our default position as humans is to hide from God (see Gen 3:9) and choose instead our "own place" (Acts 1:25), eschewing the communion offered to us by the Trinity.

As spiritual directors make such invitations, we may be tempted to stop going to direction, because the relationship has now become an occasion for conversion, which is always a suffering. The temptation to end ongoing spiritual direction, along with any temptation to place aside the habit of prayer, become the two main struggles many clerics wrestle with regularly. The last thing Satan wants us to do is to stay in spiritual direction and to remain in prayer. He hates these even more than our presiding at sacraments, because the effect of the sacraments *on the people* is secured by Christ's own promise and actions and our intention to do what the Church wills us to do in those acts.[18] Our personal prayer, however, is what keeps us in affective communion with God and anchors our faith, hope, and love in an intimate confidence that God is alive and moving in our lives and ministry. Satan hates clerics who pray, because it is prayer that prevents clergy from believing that the *routine* of ministry is exhaustive of life's meaning. If we lose our prayer lives, we lose a key perspective on life's expansive meaning; as men of prayer, we are less likely to reduce our life's meaning to the sometimes-deadening *routine* of daily ministry. Prayer also keeps us keen to *look within* the ordinary rounds of ministry so that we do not focus on their predictability, but rather on their configuration to the glory of the incarnation; the movement of God within common events.

Further, prayer strengthens us from entering the diabolical tail-spin of cynicism, despair, boredom, and sloth. Such attitudes toward ministry are inevitable when we separate ourselves from the personal reception of grace that is prayer.

What if our prayer carries no affective consolation? In such absence, faith mounts its greatest service to prayer. God sharing his life with us in prayer is not dependent upon our experiencing consolation. Prayer is dependent upon *God willing his presence* and eliciting from us a deeper trust, hope, and love for him, no matter what we are experiencing. Therefore, spiritual direction becomes most valuable. Most spiritual directors of clergy can give examples of priests, deacons, and seminarians meeting with their director only to say, "Not much is happening in prayer." To this common statement, the director responds with prudent questions and deeper listening, usually ending the hour with uncovered evidence that, in fact, much was happening in prayer; God had been very active. Here, the director is a minister of hope. The director listens not only to what we expect to happen during prayer itself, but also to the deepest desires of our hearts during direction. We are invited by our directors to pay attention to God reaching us *precisely in direction,* as well as during the hours outside of scheduled prayer. The Lord is reaching our hearts in direction as we name our deepest desires about prayer, or frustrations with our own commitment to prayer. Our goal is to be vulnerable to God, addressing our needs during direction. We can maintain spiritual direction after ordination if we live in the scriptural truth that "where two or three are gathered in my name, I am there among them" (Matt 18:20). In many cases, the prayer that is spiritual direction is the deepening agent of faith, hope, and love in those intervening weeks between direction appointments. It is, of course, essential that we persist in prayer and have real content from our prayer life to discuss in direction: *for that is its only purpose.* If we have stopped praying, spiritual direction itself can be painful—and brief.

Both prayer and spiritual direction are experiences of a sacred exchange. In prayer, we listen to God directly, and in direction, we listen to God through the inviting questions of our director. When we go to spiritual direction, we are not going primarily to receive counsel, but to further orient ourselves to the divine presence. Direction is a conspiracy with and in the Spirit to leave a cleric in prayer. It is possible to go deeper into prayer when we are alone with God because we have allowed ourselves to be taken deeper into prayer when we are alone

13

with our director. In this relationship, our director assists us to listen for God's voice, even when such a voice appears silent.

Silence is a common suffering within our prayer lives. We all have difficulty perceiving the subtle movements of God loving us. This lack of perception leads us to incorrectly believe that God is not with us. Furthermore, such lack of perception is not relegated simply to our prayer lives; husbands and wives can miss the subtle movements of their spouse communicating need or pain, thus leaving one isolated from the other. Love tutors us to attend to minor things, so we do not miss the very affirmation our hearts are craving. Saints are sensitive to love's subtlety. They recoil at any temptation to venial sin and swoon at the tiniest movement of grace in their soul, either of which we might miss or not even count as consequential or significant. The deepest growth in our prayer life occurs when we notice and surrender to the smallest movements of love from God, allowing these movements to take us up into one of the many mansions God is preparing for us (see John 14:2). Thankfully, our spiritual directors are there to invite us to follow the subtlest affective movement in our hearts all the way into divine intimacy. If we welcome and stay with the smallest of movements, they often open a floodgate of consoling grace, which keeps us attentive to God's presence. From what started as barely perceptible (1 Kgs 18:43–45), we are left full to the brim, if we are patient and hospitable to the movements of God's coming. As a brief example, consider our regular prayerful reading of Scripture or *lectio divina*. My eyes fall upon an action of Christ, one I have heard or imagined many times before, but I pause and listen or see again. In this pause, I become vulnerable. I sense myself saying, "Will you love me that way Christ? Will you heal me that way? Heal me Lord." Then, the Scripture we deemed familiar or even perceived to be empty, if patiently received anew, opens us to spending real time in God's presence. The reason our spiritual director encourages us to commit to prayer daily is so that we keep giving the Lord opportunities to reach us with "good news."

GOD IS WITH US, "LOOK AGAIN"

When we are with our spiritual director, we want to be hopeful and open to new ideas and avoid listening to any habitual negativity or defeatism. God is in our entire being. We mature spiritually as this belief deepens. A director may say, "You said you felt sad, possess a quiet peace, or sense a tension in your prayer today—tell me what God was doing in the sadness, the peace, or the tension. *Where was God when you felt such tension? How was He reaching you?*" Receiving such questions in vulnerable trust and deep reflection is essential. It is common at first to respond by saying God was not present at all, but look closer; receive the full context of your day or your time in chapel. Look again and receive deeply. Often, we end up in surprise: "Oh, God was there." Now, go back and receive what God is giving to you. Receiving this invitation to "look again" from our director allows us to rebuke the most common of all lies regarding a steady prayer life: God has left me. I recall that my director once helped me to remember where the presence of God was in an emotionally tough time in my life. I had delivered a presentation at a professional society meeting of theologians and its content was heavily criticized. I came to understand myself as a failure and wondered why God had allowed such humiliation, such isolation from his love. In prayer, under the guidance of my director, I remembered that God had not been far from me and that earlier in the day while getting ready for the presentation, I had been graced with a very strong affirmation of his presence in my life.

"Look again. Where was God?"

The truth is that God always remains deep within and the more we remain with him, the more we can receive, in serene trust, that even death (*the* sign of abandonment) does not signal the end of God's loving movement toward us. In this way, the spiritual director labors as a messenger of the resurrection when our prayer life appears dead. Our perception of God's movement toward us in our ministries is faint, and our desire for the supernatural remains unfulfilled. The director comes to us with this hopeful message, "Look into the tomb again, are you really alone (see John 20:5–6)?" The director invites us to the one thing we hate about our prayer lives: to be patient. "God is coming... wait, God will speak...endure this time of unknowing until he does. God will act...don't try to force his hand by acting prematurely," and so on. We need patience with ourselves and our own fallen nature, as well as patience with our God as he moves in ways that are *best for all* in any situation, not just "what I want now." I recall a friend who had been offered the dean's position at a college. In trying to decide whether he should accept the position, he went through various questions about his suitability and the position's benefits for him. At one point, his director asked him, "What makes you think this move in jobs is only about you?" Startled, he was then able to think more clearly about the new post's benefits for his wife and children as well.

Remaining in prayer and making a commitment to spiritual direction is a testament to our belief that "Jesus has made Himself communicable"[19] and that, through the sacramental life, he wants to take us up into communion with him and the Father in the Spirit. Christ wants to give himself to us, to reveal himself, and to abide with us. Such is the nature of love, and divine love par excellence. Ultimately, prayer is our simple response to this deep truth: Christ wants to be with us. The only thing that complicates prayer is our sinfulness. We don't need a spiritual director because prayer is complex; we need a director because we are complex. The great longing within us is to become simple, but we reach simplicity only through the arduous way of suffering, purification, and healing. In the end, the burden of *our concern about ourselves* is pervasive, overshadowing the way to attain interior peace: suffering contemplative prayer in the depths of our heart. Contemplative prayer is our commitment *to behold the beauty* of the christological mysteries until they fascinate us more than we fascinate ourselves.

SPIRITUAL DIRECTION AS A GIFT TO THE CHURCH

As I noted in the beginning of this chapter, choosing a life of self-awareness and self-examination, that is, a life of truth about self and God—in other words, choosing the spiritual life—is one of the most courageous choices we can make. Due to our fallen nature, it is always easier for us to sink into a life of distraction as we attempt to avoid painful self-knowledge. Once we are called to holy orders, we are called to a courageous life of interiority, not only for the sake of our own intimacy with the Holy Trinity, but also for the sake of the people we serve in ministry. When we commit ourselves to spiritual direction, there is a gift given to the people we serve. This is a gift too little understood, but one that is vital to all who wish to faithfully communicate Christ's love to parishioners. It is the gift of meekness (see Zech 9:9; Matt 5:5), of self-possession. The paradox is that only if we *surrender* ourselves to Christ do we truly *possess* ourselves in peace. We come to live in a stream of receptivity, assured again and again that our identity is relational, not functional, and that this communion with God in grace can never be taken from us (see Luke 10:42).[20]

To be meek is to be a cleric who has fully received his vocation, and therefore, his identity. Major clerical temptations swirl around and make us worry about "success" in managing parish affairs, ministries, and governance or finances. Governance is crucial to the charism of holy orders, especially the priesthood. However, this particular "worry" can draw us away from the foundation of all correct ordering: remaining with God. Worry over governance can consume us and, because its demands are immediate, can become overbearing in its pressure. Once it becomes disproportionate in our imagination, it fills the space that communion with God ought to fill. We then no longer seek God's face but rather seek to quiet the beast of disproportionate worry over competency, success, or achievement. When we commit to spiritual direction, we dedicate ourselves to the practice of remaining grounded and eschewing any disproportionate clamoring from our duties. Our vocation demands that we live in reality; that we possess ourselves by way of God giving himself to us daily in and through the "wound" or character of holy orders.[21] This "opening" in our being is one that establishes with ease our permanent availability to both Christ's servant and sacrificial mysteries. This wound secures us in relational ease to all God wants to share with us, as we suffer our prayer times and notice God's movements toward us through the course of our day in spontaneous prayer. We are, in other words, to find *in this wound of ordination* the *source of our prayer*. In this way, we secure our vocations by way of a dialogue with God and by the objective grace received subjectively from the sacrament itself. We are always at the *source* in our prayer; always in hope that our life in holy orders can be renewed again and again.

Worry over governance is compounded by another worry, which can only be characterized as an emotional and mental drift toward daydreaming, nostalgia, and fantasy. Sometimes, because the weight of administration is heavy, we may seek relief by drifting—by allowing our minds to stray toward a source of escape. In this source, we find relief for a time, but only artificial relief. Here again, the vocation itself becomes our anchor in reality. Entering *any pattern* of daydreaming, fantasy, and nostalgia, as opposed to the simple passing of

17

a thought or two, may indicate that a vital element in our vocation is being neglected: the deepening of contemplative prayer. Once more, our spiritual director can assist us in noticing that our distractions have replaced real intimacy, leaving us "lost" or "busy" or "scattered." The presence of such a confused state may also indicate that our current ministry is not suited to our call or gifts. Hence, we would want to explore with our director if such is the case. Sometimes when one is receiving a "call within a call," we become restless in our present duties and are more prone to daydreaming and escapist thinking. For example, we may be a chaplain at a hospital, but God is calling us to the parish or to a hospice ministry. And so, the *desires under the emotions* need to be explored with our spiritual director.[22]

A commitment to spiritual direction *keeps us* in the light, *awake* to the Spirit's movements and aware of our own interior monologues, judgments, and moods, while resisting emotional and spiritual isolation—all at the service of responding to God's own promptings. A commitment to direction also establishes a habitual consciousness about how God speaks to us, both within personal prayer and through the prayer/conversation with our director. In this, we secure an intimacy with the Holy Trinity—a capacity to receive divine love with ease—and are gifted with a true spiritual friend who can speak the truth to us about our own progress or regress in our life of prayer. In remaining in direction, we also diminish within us any of the emotional stress that accompanies spiritual leaders who preach about God but have little or no intimate, loving knowledge of him. With this stress diminished, our counsel flows more freely, homilies carry healing, and liturgical presiding carries a deep peace, both within ourselves and to the people with whom we pray.

APPROACHING SPIRITUAL DIRECTION

As noted earlier, it is important to find a spiritual director who has theological and scriptural *knowledge*, a living *prayer* life, and a sacramentally formed *imagination*, so that the Spirit has much to work with when we call on our director for wisdom. The goal of spiritual direction is simple and clear: to bear fruit in a deeper contemplative prayer life. To have a contemplative prayer life—a prayer life that beholds the beauty of the mysteries of Christ both scripturally and sacramentally—is the very foundation of ministry. As Benedict XVI has noted,

> Therefore the time spent in direct encounter with God in prayer can rightly be described as the pastoral priority *par excellence*: it is the soul's breath, without which the priest necessarily remains "breathless," deprived of the "oxygen" of optimism and joy, which he needs if he is to allow himself to be sent, day by day, as a worker into the Lord's harvest.[25]

In the context of regular spiritual direction—and the prayer that is its soul—we can notice a vital truth: prayer is not the enemy of productivity; prayer is its very foundation. If we do not pray, we do not have a living communion with the Trinity, and anemic communion relegates our ministry simply to the meager fare of religious platitudes. If prayer is the foundation of our ministry, our very minds are nimble, porous to the Spirit. As we slowly become clerics who *are prayer* and not simply ones who *say prayers*, the Spirit can more easily speak through us to the infinite variety of needs and wounds our people bring to us for healing. In secular terms, the great fruit of our commitment to prayer and spiritual direction is the establishing of creative listening in our hearts. As men of prayer, we don't universalize answers in a preconceived way, but instead, we attend to the persons before us and welcome the nuances in their lives that make them individuals.

Because we have suffered the coming of Christ in our own prayer, we can do for others what he is doing for us: reverence each person's uniqueness by listening anew. I remember my first and greatest priest spiritual director, who would listen to me for hours as I discerned my vocation and deepened my conversion to Christ. If I am fatigued and self-involved and someone comes to me saying, "Do you have a moment to talk?" with my spiritual director's modeled behavior in mind, I can say yes to the inquirer at my door and settle in to prayerfully hear their pain. One grace, among many, that is given to those clerics who stay in spiritual direction, is the gift of generously receiving those who seek Christ in our ministries.

If the goal of spiritual direction is to deepen our contemplative prayer life, how do we dispose ourselves to receive such within direction itself? First, before going to direction, we might consider spending some moments silently appropriating our vocation. Direction can help us to integrate more fully our call to charity, word, and sacrament as we learn to pray out of our sacramental character. To pray out of our sacramental character is to invite the Holy Trinity to reach us in love, in and through our vocation to holy orders. This vocational character, or "wound" as noted ealier, becomes the "weak" point of our souls through which God can enter with ease. In this prayerful moment before direction begins, either in the presence of our director or in private, we can subjectively recommit ourselves in grace to our primary way of being. In this way, we come to receive our vocations more fully. For married priests and deacons, this preparation would also include a prayer sublating[24] our marriages into our clerical vocation, wherein our imaginations and commitments become ordered under the influence of the Bridegroom.[25]

Second, we dispose ourselves for direction by noticing any lingering fear, grief, resentment, or sin of any kind, and the call to forgiveness therein. To become so aware, we are noticing the common obstacles to self-revelation during spiritual direction. Often, we are tempted not to raise the truth about our relationship with God or others out of fear that our director will judge us or that we will shed tears due to deep emotion. Instead, we avoid these truths about ourselves in a grasp for false emotional safety. Remember that a good shorthand definition for *spiritual direction* is "a process of praying and talking about what I do not want to pray or talk about." Noticing the difficult terrain of our interior lives before we begin direction and asking the Holy Spirit for the courage we need to enter that terrain is an effective way to dispose ourselves for direction. If our director is a priest, we can confess sins; if one's director is not a priest, it is a good practice to celebrate the sacrament before direction, so that there is even more freedom to talk with him or her about all that obstructs intimacy with the Holy Trinity, especially areas of needed emotional healing.[26]

Once direction begins, we should follow our director's lead as he or she encourages us to become aware of the presence of God, so that we might detect God's actions within our souls. It is a bedrock truth in spiritual direction that God wants to communicate with us. He normally accomplishes this communication from within the *truths* carried in our hearts as affective movements (joy, peace, sadness, and so on). Direction helps us to notice these movements, name them, and then receive them deeper in communion with God as he forms our conscience and guides our subsequent actions. Spiritual direction assists

20

us in gaining confidence and having faith that God gives us a word, a mission, a healing, or an instruction on what is true, thus vanquishing lies.

Once aware that we are in God's loving presence, the director discusses with us the status of our prayer life, our relationship with the loving Trinity, and how these might be impacting our vocation. If our prayer has been steady, and we have been graced with the vulnerability needed "to be with him" (Mark 3:13–14),[27] then this conversation will flow with ease around how God has been acting in our lives. Yet, even if our prayer has been regular, we may find it difficult to immediately delve into its substance. In this case, the director may lead us to discuss our ministerial burdens, personal grief, or administrative or institutional wounds. Even though direction is not pastoral counseling, all directors know that such matters should be welcomed in direction as portals into the true status of one's intimacy with God. It is vital that we share our pain and become open to the questions posed by our director. We then allow these questions to uncover the true purpose of our conversation: How is God acting in all these matters? As the conversation continues, the director will assess how much of our emotional or psychological struggles to welcome into the session or if a referral to a counselor is called for to assist in deepening our freedom. Directors want to hear about our emotional lives, but they want to contextualize them within our communion with God so that direction is not reduced to "problem solving." Also, even though all directors know that their arena of expertise and certification is not counseling, they welcome the stuff of our real lives as the stuff of our prayer. God is moving within all our experiences, emotions, and desires. Indeed, we come to direction precisely to maintain our communion with God *in the fabric of real life.*

As we continue in our spiritual direction session, we want to be aware of a few things to receive the best fruit from this time:

1. We must share all of what is happening inside our hearts during the session itself. It is perfectly fine to stop the conversation and for both director and directee to enter silence. It is vital for the directee to enter this silent listening for God's movement within. What we are listening for is the truth that needs to be said or explored. Only the "real" can be related to God, because reality is where God dwells.

21

2. We do not need to be ashamed of being repetitive in content from session to session. Much of our relationship with God is progressive, developmental. He is moving us beyond the heaviness of self-involvement and into the light of communion with himself. It may take time—a lifetime even—to come to prefer light, reality, and God to hiding, self, and immediate gratification. Directors are patient with conversion; we need to be patient with ourselves as we take one step forward with each session. During our sessions, we especially want to explore any areas of difficulty, or a grace we are receiving in faith, hope, and love. We want to discuss if our prayer has become routine, heavy, or "false," or if our mood toward the people we minister to has shifted from an embrace of compassion to one of resentment or judgment against them. In other words, we want to come to recognize any tendencies toward emotional isolation, that is, "I am alone in my prayer; no one is listening" or "I am alone in my ministry; it has no effect," or "No one cares." To push against any isolation or desolation in prayer is primary to spiritual growth, and directors want to hear about these situations whenever they occur.

3. It is good to take notes following our spiritual direction sessions. Our memories are not that strong, and the graces God shares are multiple. The problem is that most of the time *his graces are subtle* and our memories are weak, so we tend to move from spiritual direction right into ministerial action, forgetting the graces received from prayer and direction. This dynamic between the subtlety of grace and our weak memories can be seen in an example familiar to married couples, where one spouse claims to "never" receive love from the other. In fact, the "offending" spouse then recounts numerous incidents of very concrete efforts of expressing love. The offended one had "forgotten" those expressions or emotion clouded any memory of them. Either way, false barriers are set up that threaten communion because our memories are weak. This can happen in our prayer as well. "Where are you God? Why don't you love me?"

But, in fact, God is close and if we were to record his movements, we would know that his consolation is liberally given, though subtle, quiet, deep, and sustained.

4. Do not let our choice to end spiritual direction (if such has happened) become an obstacle preventing us from *beginning direction again*. The spiritual life is mostly a life of hope. It is based on our cooperating with grace and Christ's promise to remain *with us* (see Matt 28:20) through all our vocation's ups and downs. In the end, our spiritual lives are mostly about our choice to remain with God, a choice to stay in love with God. Either remaining in spiritual direction or beginning direction again if we have stopped is one of the most concrete decisions we can make to stay in love with the Holy Trinity.

Do not let a difficult experience in direction or a judgment that it is bearing no fruit tempt you to leave direction as a life habit itself. One can end a relationship with a current director that has borne little fruit without thinking the whole endeavor of direction is not worth your time as a minister. If we are "not getting anything" out of direction, it may be for a variety of reasons. Your director may not be skilled or gifted in the discipline, or you may have exhausted his or her range of giftedness. The difficulty might also be with us; we may be resisting the hard truths our director is raising in our sessions, we may be only engaged in superficial prayer, or we may not be forthright with our director, and thus there is little substance to work with in each session. We can move on from one director and seek another, but make sure it is because the relationship is no longer serving your prayer life and not that direction is serving your prayer life so well that it makes you uncomfortable.

2

SUFFERING
TEMPTATIONS

*In my youth and early manhood, I put my hope and
trust in God. I mean I trusted securely in His wisdom,
and had the utmost faith in the efficacy of prayer,
always telling myself in times of trouble to be easy
in my mind for He would deliver me in His own good
time...but little by little my former trust in God's
immense charity towards me and in the efficacy of
prayer faded away....I looked...a great deal less than
formerly, on the habit of prayer as a great gift and
privilege whereby all became possible but rather a duty
to be got through.*[1]

Here, Blessed John Henry Newman voices the struggle of countless
clergy. For those in the throes of temptation to quit their habit of
prayer, this sentiment from Newman rings true: "I looked no more...
on the habit of prayer as a great gift...whereby *all became possible* but
rather a duty to be got through." This statement fills us with longing. It
makes us want to return to prayer and await the power of God, and yet
there are seasons in our ministry where prayer becomes the moment *we
avoid God's eyes* and quickly move out of prayer to our more "important
work." To avoid God's eyes becomes a season of its own. This season
is filled with rationalization about how "busy" we are. It may also be
a season of pain so deep that we cannot reveal it to God's searching

eyes; a season where sin or distraction in entertainment has corralled us so tightly that we remain in this puny world as it threatens to choke us off from a joyful life. Finally, it may be a season of ego-empowered independence, with our natural personality or character traits fueling our "success" in ministry—leading us to believe "we have this under control"—only to have these natural energies fade or blind us into emotional or moral collapse. These are scenarios we could imagine as to why we leave prayer and succumb to the temptation to "go it alone."

Such temptations originate not simply from within the emotional or moral weaknesses of each cleric. There are sad pastoral conditions that also set a priest or deacon up to more easily recede from praying. The largest one is the apparent lack of interest in spiritual realities on the part of a significant amount of the laity. This may seem to go against the oft-quoted sentence with which so many people approach us: "Father (or Deacon), I know you are so busy, but may I have a moment of your time?" I hear it so often myself that it must be true, right? Clergy are busy people. The more revealing question is: busy doing what? If we concentrated all we do in ministry each day into a job description, the largest portion of its weight would not involve rejecting countless laypersons as they come forward to learn how to pray, read Scripture, understand the Mass, or study the lives of the saints. So much of our ministry is programmatic or administrative, which draws people to us *by demand* so that sacraments may be received. It is a very sad secret that the source of some of our temptation not to remain in prayer is the reality that the persons we minister to appear content with elementary involvement in Catholic spirituality.[2]

This lack of interest by some laity cuts at the very heart of what first attracted us to holy orders: to share what Christ has given to us. Such tepidity by a few can give rise to a lazy or waning response to spiritual interests on our part. Clergy have said to me that seeing the same twenty persons year after year at a Lenten program on prayer wears away their enthusiasm to study or for prayer. Such situations have a hidden negative effect of undermining our own ongoing formation. The cleric begins to think, "Why bother? Whatever I say to people is always 'new' for them. They never read or contemplate the faith. I can teach the same paragraphs of the catechism at all events and the content is always received as 'new.'" A future pope detected this reality of clerical life and noted it once in a homily:

How often did I look forward, as a student, to being allowed to preach…to proclaim the Word of God…to [proclaim the Word to] men who…wait for this Word? But how I was disappointed when the reality was something totally different, when men obviously did not wait for the word of the homily but rather, for it to end.[3]

These realities are noted not to disparage lay involvement in the faith, as many are committed to the path of holiness, but to name an origin of spiritual desolation that lies at the heart of our temptation to stop praying: perceived apathy on the part of Catholics.

In the face of this apparent apathy, we might believe there is no need for spiritual and theological depth on our part; thus, we are lulled into a routine of spiritual minimalism. To resist this temptation, it is good for us to begin or deepen a love of study for its own sake or to serve our own intimacy with Christ. To prayerfully study theology or Scripture is a proven way to remain ever fastened to Christ. Furthermore, it is good to remember that not all the fruit of our catechism classes or other instructions are visible to us. Some of the fruit remains hidden by the choice of those who have received it, and some remains hidden by God's mysterious design for our holiness. It is certainly discouraging not to have "multitudes" swayed by the Gospel, but it is much more discouraging to know that we have lost our own interest in prayer and study, missing out on substantial intimacy with the living God.

Being busy, in pain, distracted, independent, and "ignored," among other reasons, leads us to believe, falsely, that God is not sufficient, that he will not care for me, nor respond to my deepest human needs. In sum, little by little, my trust in God's immense charity toward me and in the efficacy of prayer fades away. All this ebbing away happens as we are ministering, as we continue in our daily rounds at the hospital or in our regular presiding at wakes and baptisms. Compounding our sense that the efficacy of prayer has faded away is the stress we bear in these daily rounds. "In survey after survey…the constant source of stress most often cited by priests is 'spiritual' stress. It is not that they are overworked, feeling sad or anxious, or overwhelmed with cognitive or intellectual worries. They publicly represent…someone with whom they do not spend time, with whom they lack intimacy and yet yearn to love more—God!"[4] How ought we to live in such a condition of temptation?

As McGlone and Sperry indicate, we "yearn" to love God more, but the circumstances of our interior lives or the condition of our ministerial assignments reach into our hearts and dilute this yearning. When one *cannot* pray, the answer is not to encourage prayer "anyway." The answer is to notice where *God is coming to us* in the folds of our feelings or the stuff of our day. Noticing God's movements that reach our consciousness is like fresh air felt by a coal miner seeking a way out of a cave. If we notice this initiative by God and respond to it, we will be led willingly back to our regular prayer life. Temptations can be helped to recede by sitting in the pain of prayer out of love, being with Christ and the beauty of his self-gift on the cross, and noticing God reaching us in our ministry. Let's now explore these three actions in more detail.

SITTING IN THE PAIN OF PRAYER OUT OF LOVE

To advise one to sit in the pain of prayer is not reducible to saying, "buck up" or "pray anyway." Instead, it is an encouragement to go *into the pain*, not the prayer. In other words, sit where we normally would go to pray and "be." As we are sitting, just feel the pain of God's absence to us and ours to him. Let this pain be experienced as a "cry" or a "murmur," depending on the level of affective suffering. We are to expect nothing from this exercise except the subtle consolation of being a cleric who is faithful to "his appointed rounds." We are saying, "It is my prayer time and I will go to the chapel."

Often when we cannot commune with God, our mind drifts to the work on our desk or to the needs of others whom we love—our family, friends, and parishioners. In this case, allow the ones you love or the work that is weighing you down to come to mind, and present these to Christ. In the paralysis of our difficulty to sense our own union with God, we allow the concerns of others or the good work that will further the welfare of the parish to come to mind. Here, there is an unspeakable grace of connecting our act of faith and obedience. "I will show up at prayer time" with the aching love of Christ upon the cross: "I [Christ] desire union with my Church," "I thirst." It is this crucified pain that rises to the Father, communicating both mine and Christ's "yearning"; even the silent yearning of my personal concerns. Here

27

we sit in a communion with Christ that feels "useless" but is, in fact, a prayer deeply fastened to the root of redemption—the cross. From the cross, Christ is addressing us: "Thank you for gathering up others in your love and presenting them to me, I will take both you and them to the Father."

This ministry of charity in prayer, bereft of any personal affective consolation, is a true service rendered by those in holy orders. Despite our inability at times in our lives to embrace prayer with joy, our commitment to sit in the pain fashions our hearts into pools of pure receptivity. If we can stay in the pain of such "sitting," we render ourselves more vulnerable to the needs of others. If we refuse to "sit" in the pain during times of such desolation in prayer or ministry, and instead, choose to escape into artificial consolation, distractions, and entertainments, we miss the "hour of our visitation"—an hour that encourages us to push through our personal pain to host the needs of others. To miss this would be to miss an embrace of the cross.[5]

But how can sitting in the emotional pain of God's absence be prayer? When we fly on planes, through turbulence, we still go forward. It is uncomfortable and nerve-wracking, but the purpose of being in the air in the first place is being accomplished: we are still moving toward the destination. Thus it is with sitting in pain during prayer time. If we keep our time and surrender our will to worship the Holy Trinity, *we are praying*, even if it is a turbulent event. If we connect our pain as an intention offered for the good of others, we are choosing to love through the cross of Christ; hoping our "sitting" becomes efficacious. "Through the cross of Christ" does not simply mean that our prayer time is painful. Instead, in the pain, we are meeting an evil (empty, arid, painful prayer) with love (our unmet desire to experience God and the hope that our love for others and our ministry will unleash some good).

Truly to "show up" for prayer is a victory, perhaps one of significance beyond our knowing. As always, we are just a hair's breadth away from refusing grace's invitation to enter prayer when we feel this way, but each time we choose to "sit in pain," Christ espouses our souls in ways more deeply than we can experience. Such espousal carries profound personal peace and fruit in ministry. Of course, to withstand such a dry spell of prayer, we would have had to be penetrated by wonder at some point in our clerical formation. Only one who has participated in the love "that came down from heaven" (John 6:51) will choose to endure for others and self the pain of praying without consolation. Because we knew such wonder at some time in our lives, we can remember such consolation and receive again through our sacred imagination, formed by the paschal mystery, the love that it carried to our hearts. God has never stopped giving us love (the origin of our wonder), and the work of our spiritual lives now is to stay in love with God;[6] not through consoling effects, but *through our gratitude* for all he has given, especially our vocations, and so worship him in faith, hope, and love.

BEING WITH CHRIST AND THE BEAUTY OF HIS SELF-GIFT UPON THE CROSS

"[There] is a dazzling beauty that does not bring human beings out of themselves into the ecstasy of starting off toward the heights but instead immures them completely within themselves. Such beauty does not awaken a longing for the ineffable, a willingness to sacrifice and lose oneself, but instead stirs up the desire, the will for power, possession and pleasure."[7]

Examples of such false beauty would be luxury or lust, and it arises within us so that we can take and possess our object. This is in contradistinction to engaging authentic beauty, which, through *its own goodness* invites us to make ourselves a gift. One way we can move our minds and hearts out of the clutches of temptation is to take seriously the need to make time for contemplating the Beautiful.

Contemplation is given or achieved says our faith tradition; it comes about through an interior vulnerability to receive love; to behold God's love and be beheld by God. In being beheld by God, one is awakened to his mercy, his offer for loving union. "Contemplation is a gaze of faith, fixed on Jesus....This focus on Jesus is a renunciation of self. His gaze purifies our heart; the light of the countenance of Jesus illumines the eyes of our heart....Contemplation...turns its gaze on the mysteries of the life of Christ. Thus, it learns the 'interior knowledge of our Lord,' the more to love him and follow him" (CCC §2715). As Adrian Walker noted about Hans Urs von Balthasar's theology,[8] Christ is the ontological key to all of reality. However, temptation wishes to move us toward fantasy; participating in acts or thoughts that are disconnected from reality. This resistance to stay in "reality" is tied up with our refusal to suffer an end to impatience; we want satisfaction *now*. The ego demands immediacy:

> "The superficial will is usually at the service of egoism. It listens to all its conflicting impulses and lets itself be led by the notorious couple: 'I like—I don't like.' The deep will… is at the service of love; it coincides with the innate desire for God. The deep will…finds satisfaction…in God."[9]

As we continue in spiritual direction, we are progressively gifted with spiritual and affective maturity. "The identity to be fostered in the [cleric] is that he becomes a man of communion, that is, someone who makes a gift of himself and is able to receive the gift of others. He needs integrity and self-possession in order to make such a gift."[10] To receive such maturation as a gift from God, we need to engage the transcendent and so defeat our habits of succumbing to escapist distractions. To suffer the coming of Christ's sacrificial and servant mysteries into our being is the crux of clerical formation. To suffer Christ's coming in one specific aspect—Beauty—is to receive a healing that frees us from the pleasure of immediate gratification.

This pleasure of immediacy is what ruins our prospects of attaining affective adherence to the beauty of God revealed: the cross of Christ. Hans Urs von Balthasar predicted that a man would lose interest in prayer, and even love, if he did not cultivate a fascination with the beauty of the cross.[11] Contemplating such beauty carries us into union with the Divine Persons. Without beauty, we become fixated on "taking" from reality rather than "receiving" from it. To be affected by the beauty of Christ—to receive his person—is the way to become a giving person. Beholding the beauty that is Christ—to contemplate him—is a river in a desert; a source of life among the distractions and life-ebbing temptations that may possess us today. The remedy for our habit of immediate gratification is spiritual depth—contemplating life and love—thereby eschewing isolation. The resurrection of Christ has made it clear where life is to be found: in faith. For us to ascend from narrow immediacy to liberty, we suffer the way of beholding Christ. This contemplation of Christ opens our interior life, leaving us affected by him and moving us to finally see the poor among us. For in praying with the beauty of Christ's own life, we are always summoned to go and find the "lost sheep." Contemplating the beautiful, who is Christ, *always* elicits self-gift. As clergy ministering to the spiritual needs of Catholics, we have a simple aim: assist persons to notice God coming close to them. We do this by teaching parishioners the ways of spiritual intimacy. As this way progresses in their hearts, and our own, we all begin to make choices out of a holy communion with God, thus living out the Christian moral life as a service to our culture.

Contemplating the beauty of the Crucified, we also become aware of our own poverty; aware of our longing to be acted upon in love, healed, and liberated. In the presence of Beauty, we become aware of a Presence with us. Temptation arises from within loneliness and alienation, dragging at the depths of our hearts. To reverse this "drag," we are called to await the Divine Presence making himself known. "The listening of our soul in prayer is not to hear a voice making a request but to recognize a mysterious and sacred presence asking for a return of love."[12]

If such contemplation is to be given to us amid ministerial life, we are invited to receive spaces of silence during our day, and to cultivate *an interior* silence—one that prevents the endless "chatter" of our own voice from defining our day, our mood, or our identity. We can say that contemplation is secured by interior silence, but so is our very self-understanding. Interior silence is the essential condition for receiving love. Without silence, we inadequately prepare ourselves to host God coming in prayer. Silence wraps us in a habitual vulnerability to receive what is being offered from God. In the transition from weakness before temptation (see Rom 12:1–2) to contemplating the eternal beauty of Christ on the cross (see John 19:37), it will be love-imbued silence that safely carries us into reality, assisting us to remain there.

The weight of all fruitful silence is known when we celebrate or assist at the Eucharist. The Mass brings us to Calvary, into the beauty of Christ's self-gift, and thus, we silently behold the meaning of this love; truths we have contemplated many times before but now come to live within us. And so, to emerge fully from weakness before temptation, Christ gifts us not only with a capacity to contemplate his love but to participate in such freedom as we celebrate or assist at Mass.

St. Gregory of Nyssa associated the Eucharist with a "remedy" for sin, noting that Christ's body is stronger than death.[13] In desiring to be healed of our weakness before temptation, we establish a relationship with the Body of Christ. Thus, we see the power of devotion to the

31

Sacred Heart as blood and water stream forth from it upon the cross. In a tangible way, we must unite our heart (who we are), with who Christ is; not simply as an idea, but in our bodies. We do this by means of what our bodies do as we preside or assist at Mass. We surrender ourselves in concert with Christ's own self-gift. In doing so, we pass beyond the self, sharing in Christ's own crucifixion and resurrection. As we offer up our own temptations and weaknesses into the self-offering of Christ upon the cross, we enter "the taproot of all healing, one's deep love and intimacy with the Lord."[14] Do we love Christ enough to enter his *transitus?* At the Eucharist, we realize that the Lord may be loved in all the circumstances of our lives: sickness, health, failure, success, fear, and courage. The Lord has entered death; so now, no suffering is void of his presence. Because of this, we rejoice and seek to remain in his healing presence not simply during worship, but as the truths of worship come to abide in us over time. Because the Christic mystery lives in us, the intimacy remains and the strength we need to assuage temptation is received throughout each day of ministry.

Thomas Dubay states, "The healing of our deepest wounds comes from contemplative intimacy with the indwelling Trinity, and the deep conversion that makes such intimacy possible."[15] Only in contemplative intimacy can we continue to receive the healing benefits of the mystery of the cross that comes from and is the Eucharist. Over time, this healing marks our moral character as a way of being. As healed or reconciled participants of the Eucharist, we become charismatic; we stand now furthering the kingdom by our gifts of priestly sacrifice and diaconal proclamation. We share in a communion with Christ that we have graciously been given and receive.[16] Once, Edith Stein noted, "The greatest figures of prophecy and sanctity step forth out of the darkest night. For the most part the formative stream of the mystical life remains invisible."[17] The Eucharist that heals the heart's affection for sin is the "formative stream of the mystical life." Such a life, however, is only measured by the ministry we render to the world in charity and works of justice. Our witness to the Person of Christ is in gratitude for the healing he has rendered to us who fall under the weight of disordered affections. We can be assured that we will receive the healing remedy we need against temptation as we deepen our trust in such a "formative stream" and continue to dwell within the beauty of the cross.

NOTICING GOD REACHING US IN OUR MINISTRY

"Surely, I wait for the Lord; Who bends down to me and hears my cry" (Ps 40:2; NABRE). When it is difficult for us *to come to Christ* in prayer, we can maintain intimacy with God by noticing when *Christ comes to us*. It is the mystery of the incarnation that founds our hope that God comes to us, that he seeks and reaches us. This mystery is fulfilled by Pentecost, and the abiding power of the sacramental economy, securing not only his coming in the flesh but the descent of his Spirit upon us and his indwelling in our hearts. Because of such divine love, we affirm his initiative to seek us out when we find it "impossible" to sit and pray. This seeking is usually subtle, ordinary, and unfolds in a gentle revelation. For example, as we are engaged in our daily commitments, we might see a sacramental: a cross, a picture of a saint, and so on, and feel moved to receive consolation from such noticing. It will come softly to our heart and then, if we want it to, it will remain and penetrate our being even as we continue in our ministry. Over time, *such cooperation with grace* can reestablish our desire to pray more deeply and regularly in our scheduled prayer time in the chapel or at our kitchen tables. As Benedict XVI notes,

> Man cannot live by oblative, descending love alone. He cannot always give, he must also receive. Anyone who wishes to give love must also receive love as a gift. Certainly, as the Lord tells us, one can become a source from which rivers of living water flow (cf. John 7:37–38). Yet to become such a source, one must constantly drink anew from the original source, which is Jesus Christ, from whose pierced heart flows the love of God (cf. John 19:34).[18]

What kept Christ faithful to his mission was this continual communion with the Father. It was this communion that held Christ to the cross, not nails. Christ's reception of the Father's love sustains and empowers him to make his own self-donation—the constitutive dimension of his earthly ministry. Temptations against our communion with the Holy Trinity can only become more regular and enticing if we block out God's initiative to find us even amid our ministry. In the Holy

Spirit, we, too, can give ourselves to others as Christ did because his grace makes us capable of such giving by our receiving love from the Father. As intimated earlier, prayer and ministry are not always consoling; they often contain the suffering of Christ's own abandonment upon the cross. If received deeply and honestly, there is yet another layer of love to be known from the Father in this pain. He is there with the cleric, sustaining him and communicating grace to him during the difficulties of ministry and the dryness of prayer. The beauty of the cross is paradoxical: upon it, we have a share in the love Christ received from the Father, as well as the sense of abandonment by the Father that Christ knew as well (see Mark 15:34)—an abandonment so paradoxical that Jesus cries out, looking for the Father, while in the same act surrendering to him in love and trust (see Luke 23:46). The cleric is called to enter this reality of abandonment, the absence of God, while simultaneously, in dark faith, knowing that God is the only reality to trust.

Some of our deepest fears revolve around this act of trusting God—acts of giving to others without thought of self. What will happen to me if I give? Will I be remembered? Will I receive what I need? Who or what sustains me while I am thinking of others' needs? Can I trust God's providence enough not to count the cost to myself that giving exacts? Christ has answered all these questions in his act of love upon the cross: while we are thinking of others, the Father is always thinking of us. As surely as we give (die), we will receive even more (rise) if we stay in communion with the mysteries of Christ.

For clerical formation to be complete, each deacon or priest is invited to learn how to enter the prayer of Christ, which consists of his receptivity toward the Father's love even while he is loving others. It is this prayer, where Christ receives even while giving, which all clergy are encouraged to enter and to allow it to enter them. In such prayer is the fruit of all ministry. This prayer enters the cleric through faith, hope, and love as lived within the sacramental life, and enlightened by the Word of God and the magisterial teachings of the Church. It is only when the cleric enters this prayer of Christ and allows this prayer to enter the cleric's own self, that ministry is accomplished in "power." "Participation in the mind of Jesus, that is, in his prayer, which is an act of love…is not some kind of pious supplement to the reading of the Gospels.…On the contrary, it is the pre-condition if real understanding…is to take place."[19] To abide in this kind of prayer is to take on

34

the mind of Christ and, therefore, to execute the actions of Christ in ministry that flow from such holy communion.

The Lord "bends down to hear my cry," which is a cry that is as deep as my being, not simply the transitory sound of my voice. As servants of the gospel, we are always attending to the Word of the Lord and the cry of the poor. Simultaneously, Christ is attending to the cry of the minister's voice. This is the triangulation of consolation that is the clerical vocation: he reveals his love, we live vulnerably in an ongoing receptivity to his love, and we are sent *in this love* to pour the gospel into the pain of the needy. Being sent in his love is the lynchpin for our entire ministry. If we aren't aware of him loving us amid our serving others' needs, we risk losing the capacity to give, as Benedict XVI noted. This lack of awareness opens a gap that is then filled with voices refusing to console and instead accuse, refusing to encourage and instead tempt, and refusing to affirm but instead condemn. To not receive while giving is the occasion for temptation to grow strong, as we grow weary in ministering out of our own power or unmet needs.

Therefore, if the prayer of Christ consists of receptivity toward the Father's love, and this receptivity to divine love remains (see John 15:4) even while Christ is ministering to others, how do we "go and do likewise" (Luke 10:37)? Let's notice Christ's own receptivity in prayer even as he labored in love.

In the story of the raising of Lazarus, Christ thanks the Father for always hearing him, thus establishing for the reader a testimony to the very communion between the Father and the Son. Christ thanked the Father out loud (see John 11:42) precisely to reveal to the crowd his own interior life and the condition of his relationship with the Father, which can be described as one of *communion become mission*. Christ is aware of this communion (see John 7:37) and he desires to share it (or *himself as Spirit*) in ministry with everyone who has ears to hear (see Matt 11:15). So, we glimpse in John 11 that, in the very process of sharing the Spirit of Life with Lazarus, Jesus is receiving from the Father all that he needs to accomplish his work. In John 4:13–14, we note that Christ wants to share, with all who would receive, this source of communion that marks his interior life. This holy communion with the Spirit is a "spring of water" welling up within us, never running dry. As ministers of the gospel, our desire to remain in such communion stirs our deepest longing, as we know that "remaining" will bear the richest fruit in our ministry. Such holy communion is not possible as *a constant state* due to our fallen nature, but participation in the grace of the sacramental life has restorative properties, leaving us with hope that such communion, as the origin of our ministries, can be *a consistent pattern*, that is, one always available to enter again and again. Catherine of Siena articulates our desire for this union with God in our ministries when she says,

> *If you have received My love* sincerely without any self-interest, *you will satisfy the thirst of your love for neighbor* equally sincerely. If a man carries away the vessel which he has filled at the fountain and then drinks it, the vessel becomes empty, but if he keeps his vessel in the fountain, while he drinks, it always remains full.[20]

Here is a perfect description of the origin of our ministry: if it be fruitful, let us keep our vessel in the fountain *even while* we minister! One could say that Jesus's prayer before the tomb of Lazarus defines the freedom we need to minister—a freedom to receive love from the Father, a freedom born of being inhabited by the divine. Of course, we will never be as free as Christ. He ministers as one fashioned out of pure reciprocal love. We can, however, become progressively stabilized from within by our own communion with the Holy Trinity. Such communion can be our source for ministry. Our own relative freedom becomes denigrated by other voices that seek to engage our souls; fear, ignorance, ego, and temptations of all sorts. As we seek his presence and power in our prayer lives, our own struggle with these rival "voices" becomes quieter, allowing his voice to grow confident and strong from within. Christ is the opposite of self-reliance; his very identity is a "relation." His heart, mind, and power flow from his relation to the Father in love. He even instructs the apostles that his ministry comes from his prayerful communion with the Father (see Mark 9:29). Our ministry, then, can be characterized as an "engagement of presences." We are present to God whose love gifts us with self-possession (meekness) so that we might be present to those who are before us in need.

We will explore ministry in more detail later in the book, but for now we want to invite ourselves to see ministry itself as being more porous to God than we normally understand it. If it is porous, then our own serving can also become an arena of prayer, an occasion for receiving the love we need even as we are giving. St. Augustine notes this:

> "For, when the members love each other, the body loves itself....But, if you love your brother, perhaps you love your brother and don't love Christ? How can that be, when you love Christ's members? When you love Christ's members, then, you love Christ: when you love Christ, you love the Son of God; when you love the Son of God, you also love His Father. Love, then, cannot be separated."[21]

Love cannot be separated. Therefore, prayer can be a regenerative agent for our ministry, and ministry can be a regenerative agent for our prayer. The Psalmist tells us to "seek his presence continually" (Ps 105:4). Besides personal prayer, the Liturgy of the Hours, and ministry, we need to remember that our entire lives are constituted by the eucharistic liturgy.

We conclude this chapter by returning to our meditation on the Eucharist as the proper source for our hope. This hope is born of his promise to never sever his holy communion with us, even if we have the awful power to do so on our own. Nevertheless, his power at work in the Mass is relentlessly working against such idiocy, as the Word (reason itself) is proclaimed and revealed to us at worship. It is the eucharistic context of our clerical lives that gives us the authentic understanding for our struggles against temptation, our battle against wanting *to go it alone*. Christ's whole revelation of redemption is a stand against our puny will's broken and disordered desires to do so. In our eucharistic culture, and as clerics, it is Christ's very actions that define our identity. His actions reach out to us to involve us in them, both for our sake and the sake of "the many." No matter the ebb and flow of our prayer lives, sharing in this action of the Savior, his living presence taking us up into holy communion, is the foundation of our faith lives. "The Eucharist, which is grace in person, *is* divine-human friendship and is thus that *regula* to which all forms of law are ordered and subordinated."[22]

Over time, if we cling to the sober intoxication of the Eucharist and the secured interiority and healing that participation in it gives, we cannot help but "rise" again in our prayer lives. Frankly, there is simply too much grace being shared in the Eucharist we preside over or assist at each day to long leave us "orphans" (see John 14:18). "I waited patiently for the LORD; / he inclined to me and heard my cry" (Ps 40:1). Dutifully "showing up" at Mass punctures the opaque wall that we may be building around us during times of a disintegrating personal prayer life. The Eucharist is both our anchor and our ignition; through it, our prayer life will be preserved as the Eucharist itself is the wellspring of all prayer, of all reality in truth. *The voices that tempt us to leave our spiritual lives famished will be silenced, and the emotions they stir will become flattened as we entrust ourselves to the greatest prayer of all: the eucharistic liturgy.* In this liturgy, we will find (with Newman) a renewed personal prayer life emerging over time, whereby, "all became possible."

3

PRAYER RENEWED

PRAYERFUL COMMUNION WITH GOD

Our prayer life is renewed again and again only if we are living our authentic vocation and resisting any voice that seeks to disable our ministry's power through lies. It is the relationship a cleric has with God that secures his identity and gifts him with a mission. This is the *only* source of our vocation and ministry. As noted earlier, in John 11:42, Christ thanked the Father out loud precisely to *reveal his own interior life* to the crowd and the condition of his relationship with the Father, which can only be described as one of *communion become mission*. We in holy orders are called to share in the same clear and vibrant way of living as *men of communion become mission*.

God acts only for the good. God acts only to share himself as Love, namely, Jesus Christ. We are invited to respond to this revelation of love by allowing God to act in our lives. In welcoming the divine action of love, we become what Love summons us to become: adopted sons of God sharing in his happiness. Vocationally, we, as deacons, welcome the precise mysteries of Christ's *own embedded mission* among the people, and, as priests, *his sacrificial spousal love* for all upon the cross. This capacity to receive our vocations as configured to discreet elements of Christ's own mission moves us to live in prayerful communion with him. To be vulnerable to divine love as deacon or priest is to let the beauty of God's missionary and sacrificial heart wound us, filling us with desire to be Christ for those who seek him.[1] As the God-Man, the actions that flow from his own being (i.e., the paschal mystery) radiate the truth, so that we remain fascinated with him through time and into eternity. By contemplating him as envoy (see John 20:21) and "him crucified" (1 Cor 2:2), our imaginations as deacon or priest are secured. We must abide at these sources of contemplation and entrust ourselves to him who is envoy and crucified, so that our ministry flows from these mysteries. The drama of our vocations is clear: Will we rely on these sources and drink from them always or turn away from them and rely on our own mind and strength?

To rely on the self contradicts all that is revealed about God's love for us and our deep vulnerability before the circumstances of life. Our nature defines us as limited and tending toward sin. God loves us not because we are perfect but because he is good. He loves us always, not simply when we are "scrubbed up" and "ready for public display." At times, we can believe (wrongly) that everything will be "okay" in our lives once we are morally perfect or invincible. This is a lie. We will never be perfect, and staying in this lie undermines what God wants to share most deeply with us: his own compassion in the sight of our weakness. Those who live in the lie that "I will be perfect someday if I only follow a certain regimen of life," will have difficulty mercifully embracing the weaknesses of others. Not only will one be constantly disappointed in the self, everyone else will be a disappointment to us as well. To accept that we will never be perfect in our vocations does not mean there will be no triumphs over temptation.

There will even be such deep healings that we become free from attraction to one or more sins. To accept our moral frailty, our vulnerability to sin, simply means that our lives are a long procession of battling temptation, seeking the mercy of God, and gratefully receiving that mercy as a gift that binds us to his heart. If we believe the lie of "perfection," we may come to believe, in the face of regular setbacks, that "I am a failure at being a priest or deacon" or to judge others to be failures in their lives and vocations. Our advance in holiness is partly measured by how well we accept and do not resist this truth: I am not God and that is good.[2]

Resentment, self-pity, entitlement, or failure of all sorts become sources of anger. We are invited not to get stuck in these sources as our identity, nor in our sins or memories of our sins; such are not who we are. Clinging to these attitudes paralyzes our prayer and helps erect a false god who judges us exclusively by failure, a god we do not want to worship or even go near—the angry rejecting God. Instead, the authentic God is always *near* (see Ps 34:18), and *hosts* (see Luke 14:23) us as *sons* (see Luke 15:24). Do not become discouraged. God will cast all our failures to the bottom of the sea (Mic 7:19). We simply need to keep choosing him over and over so that we may come to emotional rest and remain in him by way of faith, hope, and love.

It is the relationship a cleric has with God that secures his identity and gifts him with a mission. *Our identity is our relationship with the God who seeks communion with us, so that he can send us on mission and sustain us in such a vocation.* Any voice in our heart uttering a contrary identity is to be resisted.

PRAYER, OBEDIENCE, AND VULNERABILITY

To embrace this truth—that in God's eyes failure is not our identity—is a way to remain as a little child. In becoming like a child, we remain open to "listen" to the Son who leads us into the mystery that defined his communion with the Father: obedience to the Father's voice alone. As our prayer life becomes purified by listening to the only voice worth our obedience, we become established in such "listening" and move beyond any self-pity over sins, focusing instead on the needs of others. "The more like young children we are in opening our hearts to this source to receive its riches, the more…adult we shall be in opening our hearts to give to the world and its needs."³ This receptivity to the Father's voice is the key to Christ's own maturity. Christic maturity is a sustained disposition to choose the welfare of others. Rather than "keeping his options open," the hallmark of western male immaturity, Christ instead chose obedient self-donation. His identity as Son, his embrace of his own childlike identity, was the paradoxical source of his stunningly mature love upon the cross. As St. Paul tells us, "Indeed, rarely will anyone die for a righteous person—though perhaps for a good person someone might actually dare to die. But God proves his love for us in that while we still were sinners Christ died for us" (Rom 5:7–8).

Christ's act of self-donation upon the cross is a direct result of his listening to the Father's heart and as such becomes a model for our own prayer (see CCC §§2822–27). In such obedience, Christ reordered human reality and bestowed upon us a new relationship with

God. If we, too, listen to the Father in Christ, we can participate in this great "reordering," and thus prolong Christ's own listening heart in time. But first, we must make a commitment to become "like little children" so that our actions are established, through grace, upon the same intimacy that Christ had with the Father.

What did Christ do to be the listening Son he is? How did he become the obedient one? Primarily, he remained in a disposition of vulnerability toward the Father (see Matt 3:17; 4:4; 4:10; 5:19; 5:44–45; 6:6–8; 6:25–34; 7:7–11; 7:21; 11:25; 14:23; 17:5; 18:1–4; 19:13–15; 26:36ff.; 26:53; 27:46). He invited his disciples to live with him from within this same vulnerability, attuning the ear of their own hearts to his. Christ tutored the disciples in how to remain open to the Father. The key to the vulnerability of Christ before his Father is revealed in this truth: he lived out of his Sonship. For us, this means that we are to embrace the truth that the Father reveals himself only to the child-like (Matt 11:25, Luke 10:21). To share all that is in our hearts—like a humble son joyfully entrusting himself to a loving father—we need to desire to "have life, and have it abundantly" (John 10:10), but to be so trusting is a struggle due to sin. As noted in the first chapter, we often choose not to come to Christ for life (see John 5:40). We choose to reveal ourselves to idols; those realities in our life that "have mouths, but they do not speak; / they have eyes, but they do not see; / they have ears, but they do not hear, / and there is no breath in their mouths. Those who make them / and all who trust them / shall become like them" (Ps 135:16–18).

To be vulnerable before "idols" is not to be vulnerable at all; it is to have all our thoughts, feelings, and desires suppressed and swallowed up within our own puny ego. To share our pain, grief, joy, and confusion with Christ is to enter the deepest levels of reality: the only place God lives. To be vulnerable and share all truth with Christ in prayer is the very substance of humility and living in humble truth enables us to flourish as clerics and in ministry (see Prov 14:11).

In this state of ontological vulnerability, we are invited by God to draw life from his only Son, and to remain no longer "independent" and isolated from grace. To draw life from Christ is first to reveal all that we carry in our hearts. This personal revelation is an effective way to stay with Christ (see Luke 24:29), attaching our hearts filled with faith, hope, and love to the loving heart of Christ. In so attaching our hearts, we remain one with him. Vulnerability is, above all, a commitment to be radically affected by the beauty of the paschal mystery. Vulnerability positions us between the affective movements of our own hearts and this same heart's desire to rest in complete self-giving. This self-donation is not the will exerting itself; rather, it is the will being moved by our active reception of divine love. This receptivity is ever deepened by the concomitant act of our self-revelation to God. The more we receive, the more we want to open our heart to God. The more we open the heart and share its contents, the more we receive from the fount of divine love. Our prayer lives are a circulation of love, and love's deepest desire is self-revelation. This revelation is the adhesive that bonds the cleric to Christ, and Christ to the cleric.

To live the way of divine "wounding" or vulnerability, we need to become experts in noticing the interior movements of our hearts. Once noticed, we pour the substance of our hearts into the heart of Christ, so that he can carry them to the Father, the fount of all healing. One of the main labors of our spiritual exercises is to resist the hardening of our hearts. In such hardening, we no longer desire to share any affective movements with Christ, even negative ones, because the burdens of life have robbed us of the "freedom of the glory of the children of God" (Rom 8:21). The only way to water a hardened heart is to open it before the "living water" (John 4:10) and let this water flow into it. We do this by ever so slowly entrusting our hearts over to Christ, especially as we preside or assist at the Eucharist (see Ezek 47:1ff.).

The grief we bring to Christ originates from thinking that we want someone or something other than him. However, we know in faith that God's self-donation to us is our most satisfying and enduring place of emotional rest. Once we are healed of this universal error of wanting something other than God, we realize that a pure heart is our true desire. The pure heart only wants Christ, and all other desires pale and distract. We want a heart that knows that only God suffices (see Ps 62:1). The key to deep prayer is to identify the affective movements of our hearts and communicate them to him: "Pour out your heart before him" (Ps 62:8).

Let me summarize this way of prayer:

1. We place ourselves in God's presence and ask him to raise up in our hearts the places of deepest vulnerability; those places that we hide (greed, fear, lust, intemperance, etc.) or those places that carry such beauty and joy that we

subject them to scant attention, wary of tears ignited by the fullness of beauty.

2. As these emotions laded with truth gently arise within our hearts, receive them by name and pour them from your heart into Christ's own Sacred Heart.

3. It is this pouring by you and this receiving by Christ's Sacred Heart that maintains our communion with him, a communion originating in the gifts of faith, hope, and love.

4. As we enter into a life of vulnerability before Christ, both the healing of burdens and the joy of graces received quicken and deepen in us.

5. When you are tempted to retreat back into the hardened heart, immediately ask for the grace to endure the burden of love shared and to resist the lie of isolation as the "better way." Christ revealed to us that the better way is only one: rapt attention to him—an attention so consuming that all of who I am is eager to surrender to his open heart. Such surrender, and all that is given in it, "will not be taken from [you]" (Luke 10:42).

If we are to grow to the stature of Christ (see Eph 4:13) and become spiritually and affectively mature, we must, paradoxically, become like children entrusting ourselves to the Father. In this act of surrender, we give to Christ the contents of our heart, like a child vocalizing every dream and sadness. In this disposition of self-disclosure lays the path to spiritual maturity, a maturity that receives from Christ himself its own energy for self-donation. Such sharing with God results in intimacy and a bond with God that can only be described as freedom. "If we pray faithfully every day, year in and year out, we can expect little excitement, much boredom, and regular temptations to look at the clock. But the bond of intimacy will be growing under the surface: a deep, growing bond with our God."[4] Here, of course, prayer means self-disclosure in the presence of God. From this prayer of self-disclosure to the God who has given all to us, will flow all other forms of prayer, such as praise, thanksgiving, intercession, and so on.

A final way for us to remain "watered" and to resist the hardening of our hearts is to recall the pleasure we once received from prayer, and allow this memory to call us back to such activity in just the same way temptation calls us back to our favorite "hiding places" of sin. The startling difference between these memories of pleasure is clear: temptation is a lie and leads to despair, but the recollection of past prayer consolations holds within it the promise of life renewed. Even if prayer remains dry or painful, upon our choosing it, we are at least poised at the true font and not embarrassing ourselves by opening our hearts before that which can never satisfy. In the memory of past consoling prayer, we are recalling a "greater love" that can displace a "lesser" one. We are invited to push against the temptation to rest in the passing pleasure of sin, and instead choose to trust in the promise of prayer— consoling or otherwise. Only in the right-ordered choice of our will is the longing of the heart satisfied. The calling to mind of the pleasure of prayer may involve a brief recollection of a time when you received God's love deeply, when you "fell in love," or a time when you were overwhelmed with a sense of the power or beauty of God, or a time when you noticed his quiet settled presence carried deep within your heart. No matter whether we recall a past grace given, or simply turn toward this "settled presence" within us, to do so hastens that gifted day when we will be bored with sin as our place of false consolation.

TIME, PRAYER, AND COUNSEL

As we noted in chapter 1, many consider diocesan clergy as being "busy" about the ministry, leaving them no time to be interested in the ways of interiority and prayer and that such things are best left to friars and monks. Of course, today many clergy continue to experience the busyness of ministry and the frustrated desires for deeper prayer and for developing the competency to guide parishioners in their own interior lives. In spiritual direction, many clergy note this frustration about busyness and a dearth of prayer. To counter this frustration, it is good to remind ourselves that, to a significant extent, we do have control over our time. I am not mocking the "overworked" cleric here, but simply noticing reality. Of course, there are exigencies that come to us "out of the blue;" real needs that demand immediate attention only by "me." But time is still something with which I can negotiate. In listening to clergy, I have noticed we neglect one aspect of the calendar that might help us establish the time we need to develop a deeper prayer life: that aspect is the future. For example, if we were to look ahead in our calendars, we come to the beginning of blank spaces a few months out. In those blank spaces, we can start reserving time for those activities that refresh our spirit: "10 am September 9—holy hour, or visit a sick parishioner, or read a spiritual book." Time will always "get away from us" if we don't commit to those realities that refresh our spirit.

Furthermore, some of us can become slaves to busyness out of neurotic need. Such neurotic neediness is a way we can "prove" we love others, or it can be a way of believing we are loved. In such a scenario, we really are not ministering; we are not giving or receiving but are simply being "driven" by unhealed emotions. These emotions weary us. If such is the case—that we act out of a sense of being driven and not out of a choice to love—we need, out of love for our parishioners, to have someone help us attend to this pain. As we are healed, we can begin to offer ministry that comes from our freedom and not from our brokenness. However, there is one paradox about this pain: our brokenness, imperfection, and pain—if it is related to the love of Christ—can become a fountain of freedom and wisdom.[5] In the presence of our spiritual director, therapist, or simply in prayer, we acknowledge our needs and then, over time, we give them to Christ's love. Pastoral ministry can be a busy vocation, but it is not one that demands busy work sourced in unhealed emotions.

As we have noted, prayer is not a threat to our work, but is its very *foundation*. As its foundation, those who pray accomplish "more" during each day. Such is true because those who pray receive: a new wisdom about time, a new discernment about words or activities within that time, and a new trust that the primary spiritual work we accomplish is not our accomplishment but that of the *Spirit*. In short, diocesan clergy *are* spiritual leaders—if we *pray*.

From such a spiritual perspective, time is ours to order. Our communion with God becomes the source of our giving what people really need: the *depth* of truth born of our communion with God and assistance with noticing the living *presence* of God in their lives, all delivered with *brevity* of words. If persons we minister to appear content with elementary involvement in the Catholic spiritual tradition, then our suffering the coming of God first in our own lives prepares us to become wise, deep, and verbally concise spiritual leaders. In other words, our prayerfulness delivers just what the culture is seeking from us today. But we can only discern this if we are living in the depth of

46

God's own presence and brevity. Just like with Christ's own brevity, "come follow me," the people in the parish will also come to see us as worthy leaders. Paradoxically, when we invite others to know God's love from such depth and brevity, there comes *a greater interest* on their part to embrace the spiritual life.

John Paul II's prophetic statement may serve as our guide for both our prayer and the ministry of prayer we offer to the laity:

> But it would be wrong to think that ordinary Christians can be content with a shallow prayer that is unable to fill their whole life. Especially in the face of the many trials to which today's world subjects faith, they would be not only mediocre Christians but "Christians at risk." They would run the insidious risk of seeing their faith progressively undermined, and would perhaps end up succumbing to the allure of "substitutes," accepting alternative religious proposals and even indulging in far-fetched superstitions. It is therefore essential that education in prayer should become in some way a key-point of all pastoral planning.[6]

If we do not pare down our lengthy homilies, catechesis, pastoral counseling sessions, and shared prayer, we may be serving only our own unmet questions and needs, rather than the needs of our parishioners. As a father, I learned long ago that my children stopped listening to me "instruct" them about the same time I was to make my point and then grind it into oblivion. In other words, my children wanted to listen to me until I wanted to listen to myself more. Brevity is born of confidence, and confidence is born when we suffer the coming of his presence into our hearts through the prayerful reception of truth. What God is doing for us, he wants to do for our parishioners. Our clerical formation is a gift to the Church: the molding of our personality and our presence into a bridge, not an obstacle, thus allowing the divine work to proceed. Clerical formation is this gift if we *surrender* to it and make ourselves available to truth's refining power by way of our formators' ministry. If we did not submit aspects of our persons to the refiners' fire during our formation, then *ongoing* formation is still available to us. We are invited to choose such ongoing formation out of charity to the people we serve.

If people know we will be concise and on point, they will choose to come to us again and again. This is human nature. When a long-winded

47

person appears in our phone's ID, what do we do: pick it up or think twice? We want to create positive memories in people's minds about our availability to them. Such a memory is created when we listen to their pain at the deepest level and speak only what we know will remedy such pain out of our communion with Christ. The deepest level is always ministered to by wisdom, and wisdom is always brief. Being brief, however, is not the same as being curt. Brevity simply means that when *their questions are answered,* or *their needs met,* we all move on. There is great evangelizing power in bringing the fruit of our own prayer life, theological reflection, and pastoral experience to bear upon the common problems of our people. If we do so, the people will return for more wisdom and, in so doing, they will bear wisdom in turn to others in the parish.

"I don't have time to pray" is a common clerical *crie de coeur.* The cry comes from our deepest desire to be with God, but the cry can only be answered if we no longer perceive God as a thief, a "taker" of time and calendar. Being with him in prayer, we realize that he is only giving; he is not a threat, but instead bears a promise. The promise is this: as you surrendered to Christ's call on your ordination day, he will share with you his ministry and prayer, which have their source in the eternal love of the Father. Those that trust in the eternal are given the gift of time.

HOLY ORDERS AS A SOURCE OF PRAYER

"Knowing the truth and not acting on it threatens to shake a person apart."[7] What we know about ourselves is that, in some manner, Christ came alongside us to say that he would like to live his own priesthood and/or diaconate over again in our bodies. This was the attractive and stunning invitation to which we said yes. In order that we are not shaken apart at our foundations, we act on what we know to be true: participating in his servant and sacrificial mysteries is our path to holiness. To become alienated from Christ sharing his life with us by our slipping away from prayer is to become men unknown to ourselves. Of course, we can remain with him minimally by fulfilling spiritual duties. Such minimalism is not ideal, but it is not to be scoffed at either. As we have noted, on those emotionally dark days when we dutifully "show up" for our scheduled praying of the Liturgy of the Hours, or preside at the Eucharist, we keep the "airways" open until a full oxygenation supersedes this period of spiritual lethargy (see Isa 29:17–18). The only sound counsel given to one another during "heavy" days in the spiritual life is: keep the "airways" open. You are doing what you can at this time and it is good. Stay with the minimalist routine, remain open, and never lose hope; air is reaching your lungs. As faith informs our darkness and as we fully breathe again, we realize that through our prayer life, there is more than *survival* being offered; rather, we are being invited to "have life, and have it abundantly" (John 10:10).

As clerics engaged in ministry and prayer, do we believe that we act in the presence of and with a God who is real, active, and interested in us and our ministries? Our entire clerical lives change once we believe that God is actively present: engaged in our lives, interested in our thoughts, feelings, and desires, willingly sharing himself with us in the *sacrament* of holy orders to which he called us. A large part of the spiritual life is praying for the grace to know and believe that God is present.[8]

Therefore, it is good to pray with the memories of our ordination day. It is, in a sense, returning to the well of refreshment and life. As we move through our prayer lives and days of ministry, it can feel like circumstances and people's needs lessen the "joy of my youth," that is, our enthusiasm for ministry. As the Psalmist proclaims,

> Then I will go to the altar of God,
> to God my exceeding joy;
> and I will praise you with the harp,
> O God, my God. (Ps 43:4–5)

Youth and joy are synonymous, and both are robbed from us by time and sin, but as we "remain" in Christ—that is, as we dwell in the desire to share in his life through holy orders—we also stay "young" and joyful. When we are invited to recall the joy of our youth on ordination day, such joy is not attached to chronological age, but to the *eager availability* that possessed us that day.

On occasion it is good to remember our eager availability at ordination, and notice what might have robbed us of the freedom that bid us to lay prostrate on the cathedral floor. This noticing is best done in spiritual direction, so that Christ can speak more plainly (see Matt 18:20). If we can recall, or even *receive again*, some of the freedom of that ordination day, we can once again draw deep prayer from our sacrament. The endless flow of grace that is holy orders is the energy of our prayer lives. Becoming mystical clergy is rooted in the soil of our sacrament[9]—of the flowing life that is shared between Christ and our deepest identity in freedom before him. Part and parcel of being gifted with prayer flowing from holy orders is the concomitant purification that makes virtue attractive. This painful transition from immediate gratification to moral living is sourced in the *relationship* that is shared with us sacramentally. We don't simply will to be good; we will to remain open to his power moving us to what is holy. Concurrently, he is drying up our interest in what is outwardly attractive but essentially boring: vice. Of course, when we are involved in sin, it doesn't feel boring, but its true emptiness is irrefutable. If we choose to remain in *his* presence, the beauty of his love clearly reveals the core of sin to be vain. Satan promotes sin as "full" by proffering the spiritual life to be a routine drudgery. He whispers this lie to us and holds up all that distracts, calling even *within our very prayer time* that sin is worthy of attention. We can only move away from the addictive, yet boring, repetitiveness of sin if we truly believe that God wants to be with us. Do we believe that "God gathers the guilty man into His Holiness"?[10]

Here again, we move to the memory of laying on the cathedral floor: "Why me, Lord? Why did you choose me?" The very reason Christ came among men was to gather the guilty into healing fellowship with him. In a sense, the ministers of his good news must suffer the humiliation and poverty of being the "first" to be loved despite our guilt. Being "first" here means *before* we proclaim such love to all. We all know how difficult it is to receive love and healing as a gift, rather than earn it as a reward. Hence, the crucial importance of clergy formation as a true encounter with the living God, rather than simply "time in school." Only in this encounter can we find the strength to seek salvation no longer by achievement but receive it, instead, as our highest dignity. In Mark's Gospel, Jesus's deepest desire in forming the clergy is articulated: "He also named apostles, to be *with him*, and to be *sent out* to proclaim the message" (3:14, au. emphasis). No communion equals no mission. This is the essence of clerical formation. As such, ongoing formation is clear; we choose those experiences and relationships that deepen our desire to be with him so that our ministry might truly flow from holy communion.

In remembering our ordination day, we are simply turning our hearts toward the source that originally broke them open. Since being called to holy orders, can we ever forget the vulnerability that defined our own hearts? He chose us, and we let him in; we let him in, and he chooses us. Holy orders is that moment where his love most easily flows into our being, reaching us, healing us, opening our hearts anew, and most profoundly, sending us on mission. Renewal of our clerical lives in prayer is as close as *remembering* our identity, our surprise, our joy, and our humility in our vocation. "Recall those earlier days" (Heb 10:32).[11]

PRAYER AND SOLITUDE

"Man is alone: this is to say that through his own humanity, through what he is, he is at the same time set into…an exclusive… relationship with God Himself."[12] It is best to receive again the reality of our ordination in solitude. There is a great mystery in solitude: Do we really enter solitude by choosing to sit in an empty room, or are we in solitude simply by being human? In his splendid work on Christian anthropology, "*Man and Woman He Created Them: A Theology of the Body*," Pope St. John Paul II places Adam and Eve in "original solitude"—a way of being that is characterized by its expectant fulfillment in union with another. In other words, solitude carries in its very substance the urgent longing for union. Solitude is not loneliness; loneliness is evil. Loneliness is a prolonged deprivation of relationship with others; *a state, not a passing mood or interval*. Such a state can be characterized as antihuman. If loneliness continues, it gives birth to the pain of emotional isolation, which is often assuaged through sin. Therefore, forming our parishes as places of Christian fellowship is a powerful work against the proliferation of immorality. The chronically lonely person is the next perpetrator or victim of evil. Solitude, alternatively, is not a deprivation of communion, but its anticipation. Solitude is our condition as humans, even when we are deeply satisfied by our friendships and vowed lives. Solitude is our interior condition of anticipated participation in the receptivity and self-donation that is life as *imago dei*. This solitude orders us to prayer; to finding our ultimate peace in God. It also orders us toward dignified and real relationships of intimate *self-donation*. There is an inexhaustible availability within us for love; for self-donation and reception of the other. It is what St. Augustine was speaking about when he pointed out that "our heart is restless until it rests in you."[13] Such restlessness is not to be feared, but rather, is a deep interior availability that, of course, needs virtue to order it properly. Such virtue-guided restlessness is a true compass delivering us to happiness: "I am one who longs for another." Solitude is the wellspring of love, as Pope Benedict described it:

> Even if *eros* is at first mainly covetous and ascending, a fascination for the great promise of happiness, in drawing near to the other, it is less and less concerned with itself, increasingly seeks the happiness of the other, is concerned more and more with the beloved, bestows itself and wants to "be there for" the other. The element of *agape* thus enters into this love....Man cannot always give, he must also receive. Anyone who wishes to give love must also receive love as a gift. Certainly, as the Lord tells us, one can become a source from which rivers of living water flow (cf. John 7:37–38). Yet to become such a source, one must constantly drink anew from the original source, which is Jesus Christ, from whose pierced heart flows the love of God (cf. John 19:34).[14]

And so, as clergy, we still ourselves from within and sense a deep interior solitude—a singular rising up within us—an anticipation (hinted at by longing) that we were created *for* God and him alone. In our clerical formation, the Church recognizes this need to school us in interior silence,[15] so that our "restlessness" is acknowledged and ordered toward fulfillment and not frustration. In a pale reflection of the trinitarian life, we image the giving and receiving of the Trinity, and, through the ascetical, sacramental, and moral life, the distance between ourselves and God begins to diminish, leaving us free to be "sources" of such giving and receiving for others.

But, as Pope Benedict XVI noted, "to become such a source, one must constantly drink anew from the original source." The burden of ministry will only become "light" if we drink anew from the original source ourselves. To drink anew, we must *remain open from within* at

Mass, during personal prayer, and in *lectio divina*. To be open from within is to drink the "life" of God. As we remain at the source, we consequently bear grace to parishioners in what we are becoming, and we become witnesses that life with God is possible. To become a witness is the result of our own progressive and very painful reconstitution in Christ. This reconstitution is the crux of clerical formation and ongoing formation. Such formation can be crystalized in the effort we make to contemplate the actions of Christ. "In contemplating the Lord, who offered his life for others, he [the cleric] will be able to give himself generously and with self-sacrifice for God's people."[16]

CONTEMPLATION AS OPENNESS TO THE SOURCE

Contemplation is not simply "thinking about the things of Christ," but beholding his actions in prayerful love. Contemplation positions us to remain open and to receive love from God, but it is also a seeing that moves one to *action*, a receiving that prompts *giving*. Contemplation is never self-involvement; it is always about our fascination with the beauty of his love. In being so fascinated, our interior lives become more secure and freer, and prayer more desired.

Solitude—that anticipation for communion at the depths of our humanity—is progressively fulfilled as we are moved by grace into the rest that is communion with God. Yet even as we progress toward communion, we come to know its *promise* in regularly contemplating the mysteries of Christ. Some causes of emotional dissatisfaction in clergy (even immorality) are loneliness, lack of self-knowledge, and intermittent attention to needed emotional healing. There is a spiritual importance in admitting that we need to be *known*, and that we may need healing from past wounds of *rejection*. Prescinding from the need for therapy, and its real benefits united to prayer, it is contemplation that satisfies and sustains our need to be known. When this need is being met in God, and among our family, friends, and colleagues, it fosters a freedom to minister to others.

At its core, contemplation is given to us because we are in solitude, because we hunger for union. Human beings are born filled with anticipation, ordered by a longing to be "taken up" into the mystery of

Christ's own love for the world. That is what we were created to do. Of course, we need a community of faith to orient our desires in this way, but at its core, humans want God. We spend a great deal of time resisting this desire because we are weakened by fear, sin, and emotional turmoil. In the end, those who "suffer" such realities *in Christ* will not despair. Instead, grace draws us *through* weakness, fear, sin, and inner turmoil *in* Christ, like a lost child who runs to the brightening light of a clearing through a dark wood.

For both celibate and married clergy, a linchpin for being "taken up" into contemplating the mystery of Christ's own love for the world is understanding our own bodies.[17] The gift of being a man is to seek the beloved and give *all* to her. Christ himself invites us to come after him in his own search for the Bride and his subsequent self-donation for her upon the cross. He seeks his Bride (see Luke 19:10) and gives his *all* for her (see John 19:30: *consumatum est*; Heb 8:13). As he passes us, he speaks the invitation that both quiets all our seeking and stirs up all things new: *Come Follow Me*. Yes, we can follow him because he takes us up into his own *mysteries*. He lashes our bodies to his own through sacramental grace, and for the deacon and priest specifically, the grace of *service becomes sacrifice*. Here we are at the core of holy orders and marriage,[18] those sacraments at the service of communion (*CCC* §1534). Christ the Bridegroom has come *to seek the Bride and give all to her*, embodying the desire at the depths of our hearts. Both priest and deacon are spousal, in that Christ inhabits us with his own nuptial life. In doing so, he orders our actions in his, so we might serve and give all to the Bride. For both deacon and priest, nuptiality is the way of life we serve. In our ministry, we image the love that God in Christ has for humanity. Hence, even for married clergy, the configuration of our bodies *to the spousal Christ* is decisive. This configuration is concretized in the commitment to celibacy married clergy make if their wives should predecease them.

Consequently, to contemplate the actions of Christ is to allow these actions to enter us at the deepest levels of our manhood ordering it to self-donation. Such ordering is something we long for, but only realize if we allow ourselves to be configured to him. This configuration occurs as we receive his life throughout our days of ministry, allowing him to live his mysteries over again in our bodies. As our contemplative prayer deepens, our appropriation of his own gift of ministry to the Bride becomes the very energy of our day-to-day decisions.

RELATIONSHIP, IDENTITY, MISSION[19]

Remaining in a contemplative mission depends on our *staying in love* with the Holy Trinity. Staying in love with God is attained through a prayer-soaked struggle against the attractions of this passing age (see Rom 12:1–2) and its inherent idols. Positively, it is attained through delighting in God's providential care (see 1 Pet 5) and glorifying his name in worship and behavior. All idols promise the false consolation known through immediate gratification. Alternatively, the prayer-soaked struggle (see Rom 7:15) is a life free from idolatry and open to true listening, worship, and loving service.

To stay in love with God and so bear fruit in ministry, we need to resist a very tempting lie: our ministry is our identity. More correctly, ministry is the action flowing from our identity as men in communion with the Holy Trinity and on mission from the bishop for the sake of the Church. This *communion become mission* is our identity. Much pain is known when clergy enlist ministry to bear the weight of their identity. Ministry is ordered toward the spiritual and corporeal welfare of others; it is not a vehicle for our attaining a stable and centered self. Ministry, which can be altered with a phone call from the Chancery or upended through the accidents of each day, is not sufficient to comprise our identity. We are not what we do. We are, instead, called to choose "the better part" (Luke 10:42). To choose the better part is to remain with him, choosing to be with him in a readied posture of self-gift toward him and those to whom we minister. In remaining with him *in our giving* to others, we allow *his actions* to bear fruit: "apart from me you can do nothing" (John 15:5). Such an identity is first generated in the sacrament of baptism, as heaven's life is poured into us *as pure gift*. Nothing is demanded or required except a vulnerable presence.

As we grow older, our awareness of this gifted sonship may be hindered by our involvement in sin and our weakness before temptation. This weakness deeply marks us, making consistent worship of the one true God a struggle. In other words, due to sin (ours and others against us), the notion that our identity is secured by the love that is God fades, and in fear, we seek to secure an identity through achievement. We then enter a feverish life of activity, which mistakenly is enlisted to secure our identity, allowing the importance of relationship with God to fade. God is continually working to upend this mistaken way of life and come to restore relationship to its rightful place.

Considering our weakness, however, God does not immediately come with ecstasy or consolation as the soul's bridegroom, but instead comes as the soul's physician. It is as physician and spouse of the soul that we know God best, first *healing* us from within (physician) and then *remaining* with us in fidelity (spouse) throughout the course of our lives.[20]

Such a distinction between Christ the bridegroom and Christ the physician is not to be exaggerated, as he comes to us only to offer his love as healing. In John's Gospel, we read of the man at Bethesda's five porticos (John 5:1–18). Jesus invites "desire" in our heart before healing us: "Do you want to be made well?" (John 5:6). When this desire is detected, his love moves to heal (John 5:6–9). This becomes the key question from the Savior to us all: "Do you want to be made well?" As such, it comes from the heart of love. Jesus embodies the "work" of God (see John 5:17), which is to heal us out of the abundance of his love, thus giving life. This "work" of God is what we participate in at worship. Through this work, he secures communion between himself and his people, extending the mystery of the Trinity into the "world." God, in Christ, is not simply asking if we want to be cured of sickness, but if we want to be healed unto interior peace. In this full healing, brought about by divine love, we are taken up into the reciprocal love and life that is God, himself. In him, love and healing are a conspiracy to void death of any power.

If we insist on drawing our inner peace from the accomplishments of ministry and not from communion with God, all ministerial "success" will eventually hang on our walls as hollow trophies, unable to console. Throughout our ministries, we will always find our way to inner peace if we choose to stay in *relationship* with the Holy Trinity as the first responsibility of ministry. In so doing, we secure an unassailable *identity* from which will flow a *mission* filled with both effectiveness and confidence, embracing its supernatural source.

4

MINISTRY

In the book *Night's Bright Darkness*, Sally Read relates her unique and riveting millennial story of conversion from atheism to Catholicism. A catalyst in this conversion was the ministry of an Eastern Catholic priest, who served her generously as a sounding board in her search for truth. The priest became a mediator of God's listening presence. Here is Read's description of this priest's ministry:

> We arranged that he would come for coffee to say goodbye [the priest was leaving for a new assignment in Canada]. We sat in the garden and I told him about my experience…and the presence I still felt during prayer. I harangued him half-heartedly about contraception and homosexuality. But most of all, I confessed that I felt some grief about him going away. I had the fleeting thought that God himself was getting on a plane and leaving me alone again with a thousand unanswered questions. It was this fleeting sense of abandonment that made me understand his being *in persona Christi*….Of course God was not going away; of course the man before me was not God. But I knew that he, as a priest, had been and was still a channel of grace. I knew this from the way he hadn't tried to convert me but had simply remained present with me. The link between him, sitting with me now, drinking coffee in the garden…and Christ who had come to me that day [in prayer] in the church was evident….He was not a hectoring proselytizer. It was one of my first experiences of the consecrated.[1]

Radiating from this priest was a *confidence* born of prayer; embodying the truth that ministry is sometimes *being with* and not always *doing for* people. Clerics are not there to help people in the way a social worker is; our primary gift to others is our fascination with God. This fascination is our expertise, without which we are replaceable by others more competent in the human services field. In Christ, we can listen to pain and confusion and assist in inviting others to be open to receive God more deeply. Due to our prayer lives, we can listen to nonsense, endure criticism of doctrine, let people work out their anger against suffering, hear again and again the same stories about emotional wounds or failure, and more. We, in Christ, can prayerfully absorb much of what humanity wants to release into Christ's wounds. After such release, we remain present to them, abiding in the mystery of the irresolvable. Much human pain cannot be resolved, but only placed in his wounds. Once given over to him, he receives them in his heart: the sacred vessel of divine receptivity. He hung on the cross, available, vulnerable, open, and wounded. As his mysteries *come to abide* in clerics through their worship, Christ invites them to pattern their ministry upon his own *availability*. In being so present, priests and deacons ease the difficulty some have in finding him. Having the wounds of the people rest in Christ's *own*, through our ministry, enables those who suffer to experience "the consecrated." We can remain present to those in excruciating suffering, especially innocent suffering, by the grace of holy orders. In receiving this grace as our daily bread, we meld ourselves to his own self-donative vulnerability.

During the mid to latter part of the twentieth century, there was, among some clerics, a pattern of thought, which muted their conse-crated standing. In this, some clerics searched for identities befitting the values of modern culture. These values invited clergy to cast themselves in roles akin to counselors, professors, or social workers. The sacred char-acter of holy orders was emptied to welcome clergy into these secular posts themselves, or to mimic the same. It was believed that this move would render clergy more accessible to an increasingly secular popula-tion. Clerics wanted to "help" and bear good works, but not through supernatural configuration. In the wake of his living through such reduc-tionist thought, Benedict XVI clearly states the essence of clerical life:

> The faithful expect only one thing from priests: that they be
> specialists in promoting the encounter between man and

God. The priest is not asked to be an expert in economics, construction or politics. He is expected to be an expert in the spiritual life. In the face of the temptations of relativism or the permissive society, there is absolutely no need for the priest to know all the latest, changing currents of thought; what the faithful expect from him is that he be *a witness to the eternal wisdom contained in the revealed Word*. Solicitude for the quality of personal prayer and for good theological formation bear fruit in life.[2]

Seeing some clergy feign holiness or exaggerate piety to appear "holy" can rightfully be rejected. However, secularizing holy orders, or spurning its supernatural character as a reaction to such abuse of spiritual realities, is unnecessary. Holiness is about burrowing deep into reality, not escaping it. As we contemplate the Incarnation, we see that living holy orders is a sacramental extension of Christ's sacred presence in the ordinary. Clergy encourage all to embrace the mundane as being suffused with God, not forsaken by him. The ordinary is all we have; it is the venue of the ever-giving God breathing life into us. Committing ourselves *to love daily life in prayer-soaked discernment* leads us to love the truths of the incarnation and creation even more. Paradoxically, we assist others to recall that ordinary life's roots lie in the supernatural.

Thus, being a man of prayer in the grace of holy orders does not separate us in any way from daily life or the people we serve. Such a vocation has literally sent us to abide within the mundane, bridging for many the commitments of the day with assistance in discerning where God acts in them. All humanity, in other words, is searching for "the consecrated." It is not the supernatural that separates clergy from other people, but rather our broken humanity.

Our human foibles and brokenness make it harder for people to notice God, not our love of holy things. If we remain unintegrated and unhealed men who have emotional, moral, or personality defects, no amount of fraternizing with the secular in the name of being approachable will make us so. Here, we see the wisdom of the tenets of clerical formation when they charge bishops and formators to choose men for holy orders whose personalities are "bridges" to Christ; who possess the human foundation to become "men of communion." In this, the Church encourages men in clerical formation to seek the necessary healing in our emotional and moral lives. "Human Formation is a necessary element in evangelization, since the proclamation of the Gospel takes place through the person and is mediated by his human- ity."[3] Our ministry is more effective as we mature in all ways, molding a personality that is attractive and a social presence that can reflect Christ to others. In emotionally balanced men, others come to know Christ by way of *our attraction* to Christ, thus exhibiting the fruit of our time with him in prayer. What is crucial, as noted earlier, is that we are first and continually fascinated with God. As our lives become defined more and more by this fascination, we become "helpful" to persons *as* clergy. Without such fascination, all that is left for us to develop are the skillsets of the secular helping professions, skills readily available without holy orders.

BEING WITH HIM

As already noted, the essence of clerical formation and minis- try is concentrated in Mark 3:13–15: "He went up the mountain and called to him those whom he wanted, and they *came to him*. And he appointed twelve...*to be with him*, and *to be sent out* to proclaim the message, and *to have authority* to cast out demons" (au. emphasis). What is most striking, here, is that the heart of the call, "being with him," appears as the indisputable means to minister in his name. We *come* to him, *remain* with him, and only then are we *sent*. Time with Christ and with fellows in formation is a time of losing interest in the self and coming to see him and, because of him, others. The time of formation is a time of moving beyond the mind and heart we now pos- sess to a new interior life, one that hosts communion with God and becomes the cradle of my thinking, preaching, and acting. By way of such a radical conversion, we begin to be *desirous* of time with those in need, eventually finding ourselves *wanting to serve*.

By the power of such a conversion, we attract others to "be with him" too. Consequently, evangelization is secretly ignited in our prayer life—being with him—and brought to public fruition in our witness- ing to such intimacy. To be an "attractive" man for the gospel does not mean that we are flawless; it simply means that our "being with him" is our defining identity. Despite our disfigurement, others fasten upon

Christ through us as we strive to stay in a posture of receptivity toward his love.

What stands out most in us, hopefully, is not our wounds, but rather our *humility*. Such humility is possessed only through the process of sharing our wounds with Christ in contemplative prayer. The power of our ministry passes through humiliation. All good clerical formation is ordered toward humiliation; a confrontation *within our own hearts* between who we "think" we are and who we really are in Christ. In jettisoning any fantasy about our identities, we realize that our confidence to minster comes not from our *self*-confidence, but from remaining in communion with Christ's love *as power*. Hence, secular skill sets enhance a healed and mature personality but can never make up for its defects if they lay unrelated to Christ's merciful and healing love.

CHRIST'S LOVE AS OUR POWER TO SERVE

Pope Benedict noted that, because of our being consecrated, we are "property of God." Being set apart through ordination is not a conferred honor. Ordination is, objectively, a mission and, subjectively, an invitation to conversion. Through such an invitation, we become men available to serve the needs of others *in Christ*, no longer living for ourselves.[4] In light of the necessity of such *personal conversion*, holy orders as a way of life cannot be reduced to the "powers" granted on ordination day ("I could not do this act before ordination, now I can"). It is good to meditate on holy orders as a *new relationship with Christ* who *sustains us* in ministerial dependency. Seeing holy orders as a configuration to Christ sets the exercise of sacramental power in its proper context: any power remains *his*. For the priest, it is a configuration to Christ, the sacrificial victim, which orders his imagination and motive for mission. For the deacon, it is his configuration to Christ, the Word sent and proclaimed to the needy, which orders his imagination.[5] Our sacramental ministries are the actions of Christ instantiating his power and presence within the Church. For both the priest and deacon, ministry is being sent in the name of Christ. Such sending can only be accomplished by our obedience and our eschewing of isolation from his voice, his Word. Hence, both priest and deacon are envoys from Christ to the people of

God. We are sent to dwell with the people, to proclaim the good news, and to offer sacrifice in the name of Christ. As Sally Read noted, we are the consecrated. Such an appellation is weighty with self-denial, self-sacrifice, and self-effacement because such consecration carries with it this absolute truth: "*Apart from me you can do nothing*" (John 15:5, au. emphasis). Our ministerial obedience and dependency makes possible the Lord's evangelical longings in each epoch, extending his mission to people and places not yet reached.

His mission, of course, is to reveal the trinitarian love of God, allowing its beauty to move people to repentance. This beauty is concentrated in the awe-filled love of the cross, evoking the deepest response of the human heart: "Can it be that we are loved that much by God?" As St. Paul said, we have a ministry of reconciliation. If we preach the unconditional love of God, and personally reveal its effects on us through our actions, then, in faint ways, we express his crucified and resurrected beauty. In other words, through our conversion from sin—*the cross*—we receive and are sustained by Christ, our new life—*resurrection*. Our ministry, then, becomes the occasion to invite people to respond to God and participate in his own happiness and love.

To confidently understand our ministry, we look to the apex of Christ's own ministry: Calvary. Staying in communion with Christ's own self-sacrifice, through liturgical prayer, is both the wellspring of ministry and our primary ministry. "In Acts, 'the word' which the apostles communicate usually refers to the gospel of Jesus Christ to those who have not heard it...sometimes it is used to refer to instruction given to those who are already believers....What is interesting about the apostles' priorities is that the ministry of the word comes second to their responsibility to pray."[6] This early ecclesial witness about interiority for mission anchors all our efforts to "go and do likewise" (Luke 10:37) in Jesus's name. Ever since our formation process began, we have noticed a struggle within us between the pull of self-centeredness and the call for self-giving. Ours will only be a ministry of *self-gift* if we prayerfully adhere to Jesus's own ministerial apex: the cross. This struggle will not crush us if we live contemplatively, configured to his own triumph of self-gift. The secret to his own ministerial apex is clear: he remained in a position of rapt listening to and for the Father, even while suffering a radical self-donation upon the cross. In smaller ways, each time we visit the sick, prepare couples for marriage, instruct the ignorant, and give counsel to the confused, we, too, draw from the grace of *him living his own obedience over again in us*. Remaining in his love, listening for his word, and receiving his consolations, *in the very midst of our giving*, fastens us to the origin of ministry.

To remain with him *in* ministry assures us that he will gift us with self-possession, so that we might be present to those who are before us in need. Remaining with him as the foundation for ministry insures that our service comes from the freedom known *in receiving his love* and not from efforts to assuage our unmet needs *to be loved*.

We receive divine love and participate in Christ's own obedience by joining our prayers with the prayer of Christ at the Mass. Such prayer purifies our self-centeredness. At the Mass, through our vulnerable heart, the very source of ministry engages and configures us to living self-donation as our new reality. The "daily Mass," at which we preside or assist — such an ordinary event — beckons us to come again and again. In its humble execution, we find little excuse not to participate since it involves us for only half an hour. Despite its humble demands, on occasion, we still struggle to yield to the half hour: Why? We struggle, of course, because we are self-involved. The number of parishioners attending Sunday Mass has plummeted. It is the only hour *not about us, not about me*. It is the only time during the day when we are not entertained, praised, or in control. Hence, this hour of divine poverty is rejected by those who cannot weather the pain of self-forgetfulness. In our hearts, too, as clerics, we can testify sometimes to the "burden" of the Mass, especially when we have "so much" else to do or accomplish. But in faith, we know that to surrender to daily worship is the condition for executing fruitful ministry. "The most fruitful activity of the human person is to be able to receive God."[7] Such receptivity is the universal ecclesial disposition, defining our hearts since baptism and now reaching maturity through the ministry of holy orders. To participate in the Mass, as that very *action of Christ giving himself*, is the condition for the very possibility of fruitful ministry. In the Eucharist, we are invited to come to the very arena of God's self-gift...for just a little while.

To worship at Calvary and be joined to the resurrection at the Mass is the action that secures our being ordered to the holy. The deep well of the Mass contains and protects our spring of contemplation and ministry. If we allow the sobriety of the Mass to calm us — evoking contemplation — we can see that it contains the truth about man and God, such is the potent and surprisingly animating fruit of daily worship. St. Peter Eymard, who loved the Eucharist above all else, encouraged clerics to worship God and so nourish themselves on his *goodness toward them*. We are not first to be good; we are first consumers of his goodness. "See the action of God in his love for you. Then in wonder, your soul will be forced to cry out: 'How good you are O my God. What can I do for you?'...There is the fire in the furnace....To form the human person is really the triumph of the Eucharist....Allow yourself to be given to Jesus Christ."⁸ Notice that in receiving the goodness of God, we then respond in ministry, "What can I do for you?"

As fallen creatures, we look to complicate salvation when it is really before us as gift: the eucharistic liturgy. What parishioners want from a cleric is equally uncomplicated: they want a man who chooses to live his life at this eucharistic source and to show them how to live there as well. The lives of clerics who live at the source evoke questions in others. Such living is a catalyst to evangelization and catechesis. People are naturally attracted to those who are happy and at peace. Indeed, when we draw deeply from Christ's eucharistic love, it becomes our power to attract, evangelize, and serve.

THE WORD AS OUR REASON

For the one who sends, the one sent is like another self (see John 17:18–19). In our vocation as clerics, our true moral and spiritual goal is to become men who think and imagine out of hearts affected by the One who sent us. As the sacraments configure us to Christ objectively, we remain with him subjectively through the practices of our spiritual life, particularly remaining in the Word.

> Priestly formation implies a process of configuration to Christ the Head, Shepherd, Servant and Spouse (Cfr. RFIS, 35), which consists in *a mystical identification* with the person of Jesus, just as it is presented in the Gospels. This mystical process is a gift from God that will reach fulfillment through...ordination.⁹

The most crucial "mystical" practice for clergy is to be immersed in the Word of God, contextualized in the eucharistic mysteries. Such a man is a true envoy. He carries to the people, in their need, the embodied effects of his own listening to God. This immersion in the Word of God is potent, because that which is *most personal* between the cleric and God always marks his *public* ministry. Such is the case with Christ himself, as the hidden stream of intimacy between him and the Father was publicly revealed upon the cross as the source of his great sacrifice for "the many."[10]

Only a man immersed in the Word can be an envoy of its power. This power is simply the power of truth, the power of knowing that Christ is truth. The clerical mission is to testify to truth, to give witness that living *in Christ* is living in reality. "[Clerical] consecration is not just putting them at the service of the truth, but rather they are penetrated and interiorly transformed by the truth. Jesus is asking the Father to make them like him, prolongations, as it were, of himself."[11]

The work in becoming envoys of Christ is the work accomplished by the indwelling Spirit. He loves us with the love that compels us to preach and serve. This is the true power of holy orders to teach, to heal, to serve, to give hope.[12] It is this power that the cleric is filled with when sent on mission. It is a mission that carries the reason, the Logos, of love. Love is the new sanity of ordination; self-sacrifice and service are the new logic of ministry. As Benedict XVI has noted,

> The Risen Jesus, bearing in his flesh the signs of the passion, pours out the Spirit, upon the apostles (cf. John 20:22), making them sharers in His own mission (cf. John 20:21). The Holy Spirit was to teach the disciples all things and bring to their remembrance all that Christ had said (cf. John 14:26), since he, the Spirit of Truth (cf. Jn 15:26), will guide the disciples into all the truth (cf. John 16:13). Finally, in the Acts of the Apostles, we read that the Spirit descended on the Twelve gathered in prayer with Mary on the day of Pentecost (cf. Acts 2:1–4), and impelled them to take up the mission of proclaiming to all peoples the Good News.[13]

The Spirit, then, is the original envoy, *the One sent* into our hearts. He is given and dwells within us. He communicates to us all that Christ did and continues to do in his mission of salvation. Our minds meditate on Christ's actions as found in the Word, and we listen to him within us as Spirit. We see that ministry is not simply virtuous deeds executed or truths communicated; it is a *mediation of a person who wishes to be known.* Our ministry introduces Christ to others and assists them to stay in communion with him. Ministry is creative action because we know him to be the Source of life. From his influence on our minds and wills, we collaborate with others in prudent discernment, cogent reasoning, and flowing good will, thus inviting many to share in his own pastoral charity. Our minds configured to Christ's own mind become supple and vulnerable to his promptings.

This ever-increasing sensitivity to his own movements within our hearts results in our responding to overlooked needs within our culture. Here, one might think of the excellent work being done for victims of human trafficking, the work of ecological protection, the healing of Internet addiction, or the restoration of sound reasoning on the meaning of marriage. Here is where clerical formation and our ministerial lives need to place renewed attention. The stream of divine life pouring into us through the wound of ordination does not simply carry with it the familiar patterns of ministry. When received afresh, and perhaps within the particularity of a call within a call, this grace carries new, creative, and relevant ministry for each age (see Isa 43:19). When we look at the restless segments of culture, and discern what is under this restlessness, clerics can identify their response to human searching or pain. Ministry is an attempt to satisfy our culture's thirst, not for idols, but for communion with God.[14] Exposing the emptiness of idolatry in each age is the perennial (e.g., Josh 24:14–29), yet always new, core of ministry's essence. We assist others in becoming free from idolatry.

In the end, all ministries aspire to bring persons to a substantial rest in the real God. This rest is established through knowledge of Christ, leading to love of him and, once in love with him, parishioners become established in a deeper knowledge of him. This interplay between loving and knowing the real God finally gifts the seeker with "rest."

Even for those who have worshipped the one true God without wandering toward idols, their living communion with him needs renewal—a deeper engagement with his presence. Perhaps some of us have met people who study much, love apologetics, read doctrinal or theological books, and come to admit that knowledge about God is insufficient. Such knowledge about God can even be a "hiding place" from what love asks, namely, self-gift. This phenomenon is acknowledged today when we say the parish sacramentalizes people but fails to evangelize them (i.e., introduce them to a living God and not simply studied doctrine or habitual worship).

> Here the word finds expression not primarily in discourse, concepts or rules. Here we are set before the very person of Jesus. His unique and singular history is the definitive word which God speaks to humanity. We can see, then, why "being Christian is not the result of an ethical choice or a lofty idea, but *the encounter with…a person, which gives life a new horizon and a definitive direction.*" The constant renewal of this encounter…fills the hearts of believers with amazement at God's initiative, which human beings, with our own reason and imagination, could never have dreamt of. We are speaking of an unprecedented and humanly inconceivable novelty: "the word became flesh and dwelt among us" (John 1:14a).[15]

Our ministries carry the potential of being a "constant renewal of this encounter" for others. In a tangible way, whether we are visiting the sick, preparing couples for marriage, counseling youth, or celebrating liturgies, we are always searching the faces of those before us for signs of alienation from the living God. Our call is *to mediate a Person who wishes to be known.* Through brevity of words and depth of presence, we encourage the spiritually alienated to become vulnerable before the loving and living God. Like Christ, because he empowers us with his *own* Spirit, we accompany the alienated to conversion, hoping that none see love as a burden, but only as gift.[16] This grace of moving from love as burden to love as gift in Christ is *redemption*.[17] To assist persons with such changes in their understanding of what is true and real is the very substance of our own inner peace. There is no greater human endeavor than to assist others to move from sin to freedom, from doubt to trust.

With this conversion comes a new way of reasoning. The converted no longer see self-donation as something to resist; he or she moves beyond such resistance. Where once a person thought only of self-interest, now he or she possesses a mind beyond the one she or he used to inhabit. This new mind is brimming with ideas of love, creatively impressing them upon the will and proposing fresh ways to care for others, to enact what is true. This conversion, however, always happens by entering the narrow gate (see Matt 7:13). In passing through this "gate," the person allows Christ's love to reach him or her. This love is not solely a pool of consolation; it is God's love felt as pain, the pain known in renouncing the ego.[18] Receiving the love of Christ purifies selfishness. It allows one finally to see beyond the self and recognize the poor (see Luke 10:33). In seeing the needy, the convert finally turns from self-interest to service. In this purification, a person comes to "see" the poor because he is now "seeing" with God's eyes. God's vision is granted to those who let his love affect them. We will only "see" God in heaven if we have first been seen by him here on Earth (salvation has come to us; see Luke 19:9). In allowing ourselves to be seen by him (see Gen 3:9), we, in turn, see all the ones he beholds in love, the ones he calls "the poor" (see Matt 25:37–39; 26:11). In part, we in holy orders can assist people to "see" because we are traveling the way of conversion ourselves. As ministers, we offer our presence and experience to all who wish to "come and see." However, our spiritually useful presence is only beneficial to parishioners if we are vulnerable, in depth and honesty, when in his presence during prayer.

It is the cleric's hope that when others encounter him, they will experience a consecrated ministry, one born of reasoning out of love. This reasoning born of love is given to the cleric by Christ as he heals our minds from the ravages of sin. In his mercy, God pours forgiveness into our hearts. As sinners, clerics who remain vulnerable before him in truth come to know that nothing can stop God from loving. To remember not just that we are loved by God but that we are *forgiven out of this love* is the key to all advancement in the spiritual life.[19] Being loved alone may lead to pride; guilt alone leads us to despair. But being before God in truth, we stand as loved-sinners and forgiven sons. To so stand is to live in reality, and living in reality has a bountiful fruit, as it communicates to parishioners that we are approachable. Christ assists us to live in reality, to live in freedom, to live with a clear head. Repentance is the way of sanity.

Part of the clerical mission is to announce to all that freedom awaits in making this turn toward reality. Living in reality means that we welcome Christ's love as mercy. We allow his love to affect us most of all. We surrender and allow him to take us. To be taken into Christ is to be taken into his Body, the Church, where *all things* necessary for salvation are provided. When life becomes complicated, the Church is there in simplicity, securing the truth in its doctrine, saints, and worship.

The ministry of holy orders exists to announce that salvation is simple: it must be because God loves all. Salvation is not an arcane puzzle, but a surrendered heart. Simplicity, however, is not void of suffering. To acknowledge that salvation is simply surrendering to God's mercy is to simultaneously admit that salvation's "drama" is due to *our attachment to sin*. It is sin and *only sin that complicates* human life.[20] In Christ, reasoning is simple, pure, and unencumbered. It is the reasoning of a child, a mind born of trust, a way of thinking not burdened by the entanglements of sin. The mind leaving sin and coming into holiness is the mind that knows its yes is yes and its no is no (see Matt 5:37). The cleric is a tutor in the ways of unencumbered thinking, the way of sanity. He succeeds in doing so when his own mind has been reached by the simplicity of Christ's own way of thinking. Christ shares his way of thinking with us as our minds become influenced by divine love. A mind influenced by a relationship of love with the Father becomes more, not less, clear in its thinking. Divine love *is reality* so living within it places us within reality; a reality knowable by the mind imbued with love.

MINISTRY AS RESTORING FREEDOM

As we have noted, the work of assisting others to let go of idols defines the core of clerical ministry. Pouring the gospel into parishioners' pain, confusion, loneliness, and struggle with sin gradually releases them from seeking substitutes for God. Worshipping "idols" is a common activity because they bear *immediate*, yet artificial, consolation. As we abide with parishioners, our goal is to invite them to a developing communion between themselves and the eucharistic Lord. As they participate in the liturgies of Word and Sacrament, they are immersed in the very actions of Christ. In mediating such actions, we become heralds of freedom from idols.

If we are to minister freedom for others, we need to remain free ourselves through the ways of trusting God. Our role is to pray, deepen our trust in God's power, and remain available to others to mediate his loving power. If we currently make ourselves available to God by partaking in the sacrament of reconciliation, spiritual direction, practicing *lectio divina*, spiritual or theological study, and presiding or assisting at the Mass, we will be suitable companions to those in need. It is the Lord's power that frees persons from enslavement to idols; we need only allow him to purify us and configure us to himself. In so doing, we present no obstacle to him or to our parishioners. In fact, the work of our own *conversion* is the *key* pastoral "skill," promising true effect in ministry. To become a "skilled" minister is to become one who remains open interiorly, believing that the silent flow of God's love pours into the core of our being. In remaining open to God, we become *viaducts of love as power*. Such power is needed in our ministries as we generously listen to others' pain and suffering. From this stance of secured interiority, we can ask parishioners, "Where is your pain?" In this question, we are inviting them to reveal the "wound" that has long been soothed by idolatry. As we listen in charity to the person revealing the wound and its pain, we aid the Spirit by creating relationships of trust.

Because of this trust, parishioners will invite us to pour the gospel into their pain. Our greatest ally in creating trust is our prayer-filled patience. In this conspiracy of patience with the Spirit, the idols may scatter and freedom may be restored. Patience is born when we surrender our spiritual and emotional needs to God. He is our satisfaction. This process of surrender renders us available to the pain of others, since our own pain is being attended to by the Lord and others who work with him to keep us free. Rushing parishioners to healing and freedom may come from our unhealed emotional wounds. To stay patiently in the presence of those just coming out of darkness is one of our greatest gifts to them. We host them in their pain, welcome them to return, and impose no pressure or expectations. Our power is found in trusting the Lord's ways, time, and grace. He is the Minister; we simply remain eagerly available to host parishioners in their needs.

Of course, there would be no need for hosting persons in ministry without the sad reality of sin. Sin is the turning of the self inward upon itself, to seek relief from the call of God, as heard within the conscience and within the duty to give the self to others. Because love only circulates effortlessly in heaven, as we noted in the first chapter, here on Earth, love involves the cross,[21] pain, and self-renunciation. Because our movement toward serving others involves suffering, we resist love. Instead, we choose a counterfeit way of life: effortless self-interest. It is the ministry of the gospel that seeks to expose this counterfeit, assuage the pain it causes, and invite the victim and perpetrator of sin to healing, community, and worship. Only through healing, community, and worship, that is, only through receiving love from Christ in the Church, will a person remain in reality. Without such love, we slip back into the intoxication of effortless self-centeredness.

Entering the Reciprocity of Love

To counteract sin, sacramental ministry assists people of faith to gain access to the circulation of love that is the Trinity. We maintain communion with God in and through the practice of *prayerful self-revelation*. This practice is a grace-filled response to the awesome gift of God's *own* self-revelation in Christ. Intimacy is mutual self-revelation and donation, and such revelatory self-donation is the adhesive of love. It was God's own self-donation in Christ that definitively revealed love to be an exchange of persons (the Holy Trinity), and persons to be gifts to one another. The urgent desire in love, as made known in the incarnation, is to give the self in response to the beauty of the one beheld. All love wishes to reveal itself, to be received and then, in turn, given to the one who first elicited our self-giving. In the realm of Christian spirituality and holiness, this mutual self-giving is the core of prayer. "True, *eros* tends to rise 'in ecstasy' towards the Divine, to lead us beyond ourselves; yet for this very reason it calls for a path of ascent, renunciation, purification and healing....Yet *eros* and *agape*—ascending love and descending love—can never be completely separated. The more the two, in their different aspects, find a proper unity in *the one reality of love*, the more the true nature of love in general is realized."[22]

As clergy, we assist parishioners to enter this reciprocity of love through our sacramental, proclaimed, and charitable ministries. Through ministry, the truth and beauty of God's love for each person, once obstructed by sin, *emerges* to invite parishioners to trust him with their lives. To enter and remain within this circulation of love between man and God *is reality*. To live in reality is to be with God in peace. To be called to invite others to *enter reality* marks the deepest beauty of clerical ministry, and its most urgent purpose. If we commit ourselves to remain in reality, to stay fastened to God in love, then that which is most *personal* to us (our own conversions) will have a dramatic *public* effect: the conversion of others.[23]

Our Freedom

Because our ministries can be instruments of conversion in others doesn't mean we bear the burden of being "perfect." In fact, to be "perfect, therefore, as your heavenly Father is perfect" (Matt 5:48) simply means that we are called to love and keep trying to love *all*, even those whom we consider our "enemies." In broader terms, to be perfect means to love in a manner that doesn't pick and choose; welcoming and evangelizing all without discrimination, just as the sun shines on the good and bad alike (see Matt 5:45). Consequently, perfection is not about mastering the art of error-free ministry or even surmounting our character flaws completely; it means hosting persons without discrimination. Suffering the coming of all—many with insurmountable sufferings or bearing sins that personally repulse us or try our patience—is the gift that holy orders can bring to our culture. To do such hosting is an expression of the mind of Christ, a mind we wish to inhabit as our own (see 1 Cor 2:16). Without such nondiscrimination in ministry, we cannot be faithful to our vocations. This kind of perfection is not easy to attain. To become a cleric who "hosts" others is part of our overall moral healing that Christ is accomplishing through our own participation in the healing sources of Catholicism.

Alternatively, moral perfectionism keeps us captured in a mirror of relentless self-examination. In moral perfectionism, there is little room to host anyone other than the self and our achievements (or our ruminations over failure). Such perfectionism is healed in deeper contemplative prayer. Contemplative prayer heals our disfigured image of God, and gifts us with the true image of God in relation to our sins. The neurotic perfectionist believes that his sinful behavior *prevents God from loving him*, and so he chooses a path of self-improvement, or ultimately, self-defeat. The ill-conceived theory is that once the perfectionist believes himself to be "accomplished," he can enter the presence of God again. This, of course, is futile. Sin does not chase God away from us; it only masks how truly close he is. Sin calls to God. Perfectionism enslaves us to "get *everything* right." Consequently, we become isolated from others and God, thus giving rise to undue emotional stress. As our prayer deepens, we come to see that Christ is the only one to choose rightly all the time. We can, however, share in some of his wisdom and strength if we allow him to take possession of souls.

This possession yields humility in us, but never error-free ministry or personal sinlessness.

Besides moral perfectionism, we also listen to other lies within our own hearts about ministry, such as the following: "I have to hurry all day so as not to disappoint anyone," or "If I make a mistake, people will reject God and leave the Church," or "If I don't answer all people's questions accurately and convincingly, they will go to another parish or denomination." Also, we may carry burdensome imaginings about productivity: "How am I going to get all this done?" Such a question carries hints that we feel alone in ministry, perhaps even alienated from God. The opposite temptation may also burden us ("I feel overwhelmed, so I delegate work disproportionately"), thus masking a laziness or minimalism in the execution of pastoral duties.

Beyond these personal burdens that arise within us because of our personalities or past emotional wounds, there is an external source of stress caused by what can only be called a culture of isolation or apathy among and between clerics. This culture exists where little or no affirmation passes between priests and deacons, deacons and deacons, or priests and priests. In this dearth of healthy love and affirmation, a man may go seeking his own affirmation, drawing attention to himself or acting out in inappropriate ways that may lead to further isolation. Such "attention getters" act out of pain. Of course, some may be acting out of pride, but mostly the culture of isolation breeds attention getting. Whereas, within a culture of love, we can all settle into our place and act out of our gifts, not our neediness. Without brotherly affirmation, it is easy to live a life of compound isolation, where we understand ourselves to be "independent contractors" simply doing our duty.

In all these ways, the cleric is threatened in his freedom. Ministry is a bi-level life, wherein we ask the Lord to protect our freedom so that we might be available to assist parishioners in their struggle to retain their own.

5

UNITED IN HOLY ORDERS

Throughout the history of the Church, there have been times when interiority has been lost.[1] In response, God raises up those who renew the interior life, reestablishing the proper order of happiness. This order correctly flows when we simply choose to be with Christ, contemplate his love, and from within this contemplation, receive a mission. Rejuvenation of ministry is simply being with him, letting him affect us, and sharing with others what he has given to us. And such rejuvenation of ministry always takes place within the real context of the man who is ministering, be that a celibate way of life or the way of marriage.

PRIESTLY CELIBACY

When a man is called to sacrifice marriage for the priesthood, he is simultaneously called to become a "mystic."[2] Without becoming a man fascinated with the Holy, the need for erotic fulfillment goes in search of erroneous places of rest, like a homeless man looking for shelter. There is only *one* reason God calls a man to celibacy: he wants the man's full attention, so he can satisfy the man's need for love. This received love is not simply for a man's personal consolation, since such receptivity is further ordered to overflow in love of neighbor as ministry. The mysticism of celibacy proclaims that in binding one's life to

God's infinitely generous love, a man gives himself away with universal love for the "many" (see Matt 26:28).

Perhaps out of embarrassment over the intimacy implied in celibacy, some clerics like to reduce its meaning to pragmatics, that is, it renders them more available to minister or allows easier management of priestly assignments for bishops, and so on. Such a reduction is dangerous. The Church does not want bachelors or workaholics or "shy" men using their "single" state to earn a living from the Church. History has shown that, after a while, such men will direct their need to assuage loneliness in pathological or sinful ways. Making the transition from bachelor to priestly commitment tutors a man to correctly receive love from God and, sometimes from God *alone*, and to do so in peace. To become a man fascinated with the Holy may take many years as the superficial elements of "popular Western culture" are "exorcised." Only commitment to a way of life centered in prayer and mercy toward others can liberate a priest from such superficial elements.

To underscore the vitality of a contemplative life for the celibate diocesan priest is not to make a category mistake and foist upon him the life of a monk. Indeed, without deep interiority and an identity that rests in communion with God, there can be no *sending* into ministry. In fact, to "take" ministry without being "sent" by God within an ecclesial context configures priestly life as counterfeit. If celibate ministry does not flow from communion with God in personal prayer and sacramental engagement, then from what source does such single-hearted service flow?

It is a vocational necessity for a priest to have, as primary mental and affective nourishment, a celibate mystic imagination firmly rooted in his character as he attends to the paschal mystery of Christ. Contemplating the paschal mystery constitutes the priest's main object in affective spiritual development, along with an integrated intellectual, fraternal, and ministerial life. If one is to sacrifice "the woman" and attend to the transcendent in erotic ways, then it is only God who can assuage and inhabit the "ache" of that sacrifice. Celibacy is, in fact, the privileged opportunity for this man who aches to encounter and remain with Christ. This ache, of course, is not simply the absence of "the woman"; it is the pain of humankind separated from his rightful place as freely receiving and giving love to God without the obstruction of sin. The ache is not just for marriage; celibacy reveals the ache as abiding even deeper in the human core. It is an urgent longing for God and God alone. The celibate, then, is called into the privileged vocation to experience the ache of humankind for God, the original object of erotic longing. Hence, in this broken world, in our own limited and finite capacities, a celibate needs contemplative prayer and a life of adoring the beauty of God in ways that affect his deepest center, thus gifting him with rest, healing, and profound love.

MARRIAGE AND HOLY ORDERS

The married cleric aches for his wife and finds certain rest in communion with her, but as both his and her prayer life deepen (she often more quickly than he), it soon becomes evident that marriage is not sufficient for the human person. The heart is restless for its true and eternal nuptial destiny in God. The romantic language of the young married couple—that is, "you are my everything" or "I adore you"—is exposed as more expressive of deeper longings than first understood. All spouses would break under the intrinsic expectations of a marriage that sought the spouse as "god"; as "perfect" as the one "who fulfills me." Such language of desire expresses the spouse's search for God, not a man or a woman. Hence, a married life content with "shallow prayer," as St. John Paul II called it, places the couple at risk. The risk is that once the human exchange of bodies, emotions, and dreams reaches its breaking point, the shallow pray-ers will look elsewhere for satisfaction. Here, one may think there must be a "better" spouse "out there," that is, "I must have made a mistake, I should leave my spouse and start again to find fulfillment." Not only will those with a shallow prayer life inexorably seek "perfection," they will do so in a manner that damages and destroys the very beauty first intuited in one another. The answer to restlessness is not abandonment, a fresh start, the dissolving of bonds, or the leaving of persons; the answer for couples is to move from shallow prayer to depth. It is the invitation to go deep, not broad; it is the ironic invitation to meet the celibate in contemplative prayer. Now, the husband, the wife, and celibate meet in God.

Married couples witnessing the movement of a deacon and his wife from shallow prayer to substantive prayer is one of the greatest gifts the married clergy gives to the Church. Their testimony to such a life of prayer is a clear prophecy that any emotional emptiness that arises within married life in the West cannot be healed simply by finding a "new" spouse, profession, hobby, or travel destination. As the celibate priest witnesses to God's providential love for all humankind in his sacrifice of the wife, so the deacon and his wife are asked to sacrifice the search for perfection in persons or realities other than God. Moving from shallow prayer to substantive prayer allows God to prove that *he is enough for couples in their love for one another.*

For deacon formation programs to miss taking the man and his wife from superficial to contemplative prayer is to deny the man's ministry its greatest prophetic utterance: "My wife, achievements, and escapist pursuits are not enough. Only God is enough." Here, the deacon gifts other married men and women with a truly evangelical message, one delivered to the core of society and family life. The mission of the deacon in relation to the family is profoundly cyclical: the deacon is raised in a family as a boy and, statistically, will fall in love and begin his own family before the call to diaconate is discerned,[3] and then, after ordination, other families will call out to him to have his ministry bless their communion in many ways.

As an effect of the grace of holy orders, a man becomes "useful" to families by his own character conversion through diaconal formation, and in the postordination gift of being a man who participates in the servant mysteries of Christ, the sent-servant. Since his ordination, the deacon has been lacerated by Christ's own mission to "find the lost." Ordination has opened the man to being affected by Christ's own compassionate gaze as it rests upon those in pain. It is from this "opened" and altered man, one wounded by divine love, that a deeper communion with God may be mediated to the family. This communion may be attained and sustained by way of a deacon praying with them, serving their familial needs through the works of mercy, and guiding them through their difficulties out of his own Word-saturated mind and heart.

For the deacon in his own family, spousal and paternal love are taken up into Christ's own servant mysteries. Diaconate is not bestowed upon an entire family, but upon a man who receives holy orders and now loves and governs his home as one so configured. His spousal and paternal mind and heart are now affected by the diaconal imagination—a mind opened to the mystery of Christ's own mission to serve the suffering. Therefore, if the deacon participated in sound clerical formation, a wife will fall more in love with her husband after ordination. This "sent-servant" has become even more "spousal" and available to serve her. Unfortunately, men whose diaconal formation has been reduced to academic studies and pastoral practicums leave themselves unscorched by Christ's own love; thus, their character and behavior may still reflect a cultural identity rather than intimate discipleship. Such a state instills deep insecurity within the wife, as her husband tries to build his diaconate not upon any communion of relationships, but upon activities, busyness, and achievements. This knowledgeable but unformed and unhealed husband now attempts to possess an identity through accomplishments.

Alternatively, the man who risked all and entered formation so that it could enter him, possesses the capacity to integrate—that is, to suffer—all his sacraments into his own body. He understands clearly that Christ normally gives fruit to ministry only when a deacon is first open to his own healing. The clear mark that a man has been config-ured to Christ's own servant mysteries after ordination is that he bears the suffering of his full life within himself and does not lay it upon his wife or children. For this to have happened, the deacon has to have been converted from self-centeredness, individualism, and ministerial careerism to living life as a sincere gift.

The well-formed deacon realizes that the demands placed on him as spouse, father, and deacon are fully capable of integration because it is not his ministry he is executing; it is Christ's actions inhabiting him. The paradoxical complexity of the simple diaconal life is unlivable only by men who are unhealed emotionally or spiritually—ones using ministry to "discover" themselves or "move on to the next achieve-ment" of their lives.

Within the collaborative ministerial web of diaconal service, a deacon coordinates his ministry with the bishop, priests, religious, and the laity of the diocese. There is no reason to presume that any one man's presence is essential in responding to the needs of the Church. We know this is true by evidence of the speed in which diaconal duties are continued by a successive deacon following a ministerial transfer. Of course, as individual persons, each is irreplaceable, but the ministry goes on. The Body of Christ, the Church, assists the deacon in exercis-ing his ministry as surely as the deacon assists others when necessary.

Spiritual and emotional health dictates that Christ is the only essen-tial ministerial presence, and his grace transcends any one deacon. As we noted earlier, personal identity for those in holy orders flows from relationships, not ministry: relationships with the Trinity, one's family, and the bishop. When one has union with these persons, then the ministry—the actions that one does in the name of Christ—will not be unduly heavy or time-consuming, since their effect is brought about by the "holy" communion maintained with these persons and not the time spent away from home. Saints heal with a word, not a speech. Holy people heal with a blessing, not an indefinite association with the needy one. It is God's power—not our efforts—that "makes things happen." His power occupies the core effectiveness of any cleric's mission.

For both the celibate and the married clergyman, ministry results from him guarding the communion to which he has surrendered himself—the Church and its needs, primarily for the celibate, and wife and children primarily for the espoused cleric. But for both ways of living mission, however, it is spousal love that marks each man's character. For both are being taken up into Christ's own way of loving his Bride, the Church. For the deacon, he gives himself to his wife in Christ and, from such communion under the commission of the bishop, he ministers the Word to those in need. For the celibate priest, his fitting celibacy marks his and the Church's imagination with the complete sacrifice of Christ the Bridegroom. It is, however, this image of Christ the Bridegroom that marks holy orders as a whole. The celibate, from the beginning, images the exclusive love of Christ toward the Church; the married cleric is an emblem of such love in his love for his wife, but, even still, the celibate gift awaits if she would predecease him. In the end, holy orders is haunted by the spousal love of Christ, either in the form of man and wife, or in the form of celibate sacrifice revealing the "great mystery" (see Eph 5). Both the wife and the Church have a right to be loved in a total and exclusive manner;[4] hence, all cleric-spouses are configured to Christ's ultimate priestly spousal act of self-donation on Calvary, now known to the Church in the Eucharist, where sacrifice (priesthood) is founded on the service (diaconal) of Christ himself.

THE BROTHERHOOD OF OPEN HANDS

People want to be loved by Christ and want to know Christ's love concretely. This desire is satisfied by the gift of the Eucharist—the gift of Christ's own actions of love toward the Bride. These actions are still vibrantly among us, extended in time by divine providence. This concrete love is mediated by both the ministry of those in holy orders and in their very being. For the cleric, our being with the people is grace-filled if we are in an ongoing disposition of vulnerability toward Christ's healing power. In our suffering Christ's love in our own bodies, we, as clerics, can extend grace by simply being with parishioners. If we do not share all our thoughts, feelings, and desires with Christ in our personal prayer, our spiritual life will not simply rest at any given plateau but will descend and fade away.

The anchor for our personal prayer life is found in the steady and objective reality of the eucharistic liturgy. Both the eucharistic species, and those who preside and assist at these mysteries, have been changed by the holy descent that is *epiclesis*. The Holy Spirit has wounded our hearts as clerics, *opening* the priest's hands to receive chrism, and *opening* the hands of the deacon to receive the gospel. Of course, this *office of open hands* assures the Bride that she will receive the sacrificial love and service of Christ. In the mystery that is holy orders, the opening of the hands establishes the posture of clerics toward the power of Christ. This *mystery of open hands* becomes the yes of the cleric permitting Christ to engulf him in his own sacred actions of sacrifice and service.

The symbol of hands receiving is complemented by the symbol of hands bestowing, that of the bishop's own hands upon the head of both priest and deacon.[5] Here, the complementary lives of priests and deacons join under the authority of the bishop, whose singular office, in Christ, becomes the uniting source of holy orders itself. The laying on of hands (see Acts 6:6; 13:3) surely dispenses the Holy Spirit. In this bestowal, the cleric's mind and will become permanently available to Christ and his mission. The laying on of hands implies one becoming a sacrifice, being healed, and, of course, being sent or consecrated (see Num 8:5ff.; Lev 3:2; 1:4; Acts 6:6; 13:3; Luke 4:40).

In this convergence of open hands and receptive hearts, the priest and deacon find their brotherhood. In some quarters of the Church, there has been tension between the priest and the deacon in parishes. These tensions simply represent the emotional brokenness of human beings. Thus, the tension is not in the relationship between priest and deacon as brothers of the open hands, but in the disease of personal sin and ignorance. More practically, some of the tension is born in ministerial incompetence, idiosyncratic personality struggles, and poor clerical formation. As such, there is hope since competence can be taught, personalities somewhat healed, and formation reestablished, thus allowing for priest/deacon relationships to develop in future years. An irenic and fruitful cooperative mission is worth pursuing, so that a fuller symbol of Christ's mission as "service become sacrifice" can be clearly seen in each diocese. Just like the symbol of Christ's great love in the Eucharist is clearly expressed when all receive the precious body and blood in holy communion, so the ministry of Christ is clearly expressed in its fullness when all three grades of holy orders labor together to proclaim Christ's great love. The Church is itself the sacrament of communion, and we, its ministers, better experience that communion when we remain in sustained communion with Christ, and from that fount of healing, abide in communion with our fellow workers in the vineyard.

CONCLUSION

The prayer life of the cleric is the irreplaceable and vibrant center of his inner peace, inspiration, and spiritual well-being. Very simply, his prayer life is his oxygen.[6] Without this fresh air, the cleric loses his breath, becomes sluggish, and due to the pain caused by being spiritually breathless, becomes self-involved. We began this book promoting spiritual direction as the golden thread of holiness in the life of any cleric. It, along with regular confession, daily prayer, and vulnerability to God's movements in us during ministry, will help secure our necessary and living relationship with Christ.

The spiritual life is synonymous with who we are. To lose our communion with the Holy Trinity is to lose the *very meaning of our existence*, hence the mountains of publications, lectures, retreats, and audio resources aimed at clerics pouring out of the Church. This avalanche of resources bears with it a profound prayerful hope that we don't fall out of love with God, as well as the Church's love toward us, which encourages us to remain in him (see John 15:4). I add this small project to such hope and such love.

NOTES

1. SPIRITUAL DIRECTION

1. Jean D'Elbee, *I Believe in Love* (Manchester: Sophia, 2001), 109–10, quoting Jean Pierre de Caussade.

2. Of course, we come to know God in faith through our senses, but since they are weakened through sin, we easily attend to other realities that more immediately garner our attention, see *CCC* §§31–35.

3. William May, *Marriage: The Rock on Which the Family Is Built*, rev. exp. ed. (San Francisco: Ignatius Press, 2009), 38–39.

4. Michael Paul Gallagher, *Faith Maps: Ten Religious Explorers from Newman to Joseph Ratzinger* (Mahwah, NJ: Paulist Press, 2010), 71.

5. Matthew Levering, *Christ and the Catholic Priesthood* (Mundelein: Hillenbrand, 2010), 180.

6. Joseph Ratzinger, *God and the World: A Conversation with Peter Seewald* (San Francisco: Ignatius Press, 2002), 332–36, at 333.

7. Love of one's future spouse can begin as an immediate "falling," or it can develop over time as when one is suffused with her presence since childhood, slowly developing until one "marries the girl next door." These ways of love can happen with God as well. Either way, there will be a time when the presence of the beautiful will "demand" a choice to give what one is not quite ready to yield. In this is the suffering Joseph Ratzinger is meditating on above.

8. St. Augustine, *Confessions*, bk. 8, chap. 11, no. 26.

9. John Crosby, *The Personalism of John Henry Newman* (Washington, DC: CUA Press, 2014), 45.

10. See James Keating, "Theology as Thinking in Prayer," *Chicago Studies* 53, no. 1 (2014).

11. J. Brian Bransfield, *Overcoming Pornography Addiction: A Spiritual Solution* (Mahwah, NJ: Paulist Press, 2013), 38.

12. Of course, I am positing this statement from the perspective of an affectively healthy condition. There are those whose image of God is distorted through suffering, and perhaps see prayer as emotionally unsafe. This condition would invite needed psychological and spiritual healing.

13. See Donald Haggerty, *The Contemplative Hunger* (San Francisco: Ignatius Press, 2016), 38–39.

14. Benedict XVI, *A School of Prayer* (San Francisco: Ignatius Press, 2013), 31–32.

15. It remains true that the contemporary masters of spiritual direction are William Barry and William Connolly, *The Practice of Spiritual Direction*, rev. ed. (New York: HarperCollins, 2009). If one is to understand both what it means to be a director and to be directed, their book is the primary well of wisdom. I also recommend Donald Haggerty, *The Contemplative Hunger* (San Francisco: Ignatius Press, 2016) as a primary source for understanding the anthropology of prayer, that is, prayer as our deepest identity. Finally, Fr. Timothy Gallagher, OMV, has definitively restored the skills of Ignatian discernment in the twenty-first century. To understand both direction and being directed, his books are required as well. See Timothy Gallagher, *The Discernment of Spirits* (New York: Crossroad, 2005); and *A Handbook for Spiritual Directors* (New York: Crossroad, 2017).

16. "Prayer is essentially what God does....And what God is doing for us is giving us the divine Self in love." Ruth Burrows, *Essence of Prayer* (Mahwah, NJ: Hiddenspring, 2006), 1.

17. Benedict XVI, "Homily at World Youth Day" (Sunday, July 20, 2008).

18. "The very holiness of priests is of the greatest benefit for the fruitful fulfillment of their ministry. While it is possible for God's grace to carry out the work of salvation through unworthy ministers, God ordinarily prefers to show his wonders through those men who are more submissive to the impulse and guidance of the Holy Spirit and who, because of their intimate union with Christ and their holiness of life, are able to say with St. Paul: 'It is no longer I who live, but Christ who lives in me' (Gal 2:20)" (*Presbyterorum Ordinis* 12).

19. Joseph Cardinal Ratzinger, *Behold the Pierced One: An Approach to a Spiritual Christology*, trans. by G. Harrison (San Francisco: Ignatius Press, 1986), 30.

20. See Eugene Florea, *The Priest's Communion with Christ: Dispelling Functionalism* (Omaha: IPF Publications, 2018).

21. See James Keating, *The Heart of the Diaconate* (Mahwah, NJ: Paulist Press, 2015), 49–59.

22. Haggerty, *The Contemplative Hunger*, 169.

23. Benedict XVI, "Meeting with the Priests and Permanent Deacons of Bavaria in the Cathedral of St. Mary and St. Corbinian in Freising," September 14, 2006.

24. Sublation in the sense that one reality, marriage, is taken up into another, holy orders, without the former vanishing into the latter.

25. For a thorough treatment of this vital christological identity, see Brant Pitre, *Jesus the Bridegroom: The Greatest Love Story Ever Told* (New York: Image, 2018).

26. Spiritual direction is not psychological counseling, but spiritual direction can assist in emotional healing as it encourages the directee to reveal all before the loving gaze of the Father, whose own heart, Christ, desires healing for his beloved people. See CCC §1508, and Mary Healy, *Healing* (Huntington, IN: Our Sunday Visitor, 2015), 59; Thomas Berg, *Hurting in the Church: A Way Forward for Wounded Catholics* (Huntington, IN: Our Sunday Visitor, 2017); James Keating, ed., *Seminary Theology III: Seminary Formation and Psychology* (Omaha: IPF Publications, 2013).

27. See James Keating, "Interior Living as a Condition for Clerical Mission," *Chicago Studies* 55, no. 2 (Fall 2016): 89–97.

2. SUFFERING TEMPTATIONS

1. Louis Bouyer, *Newman: An Intellectual & Spiritual Biography of John Henry Newman* (San Francisco: Ignatius Press, 2011), 303.

2. Claire Gecewicz, "Most U.S. Catholics Rely Heavily on Their Own Conscience for Moral Guidance," Pew Research Center, April 19, 2016, http://www.pewresearch.org/fact-tank/2016/04/19/most-catholics-rely-heavily-on-their-own-conscience-for-moral-guidance/. "Despite Pope Francis' overwhelming popularity, only

about one-in-ten American Catholics say they turn to the pope 'a great deal' for guidance on difficult moral questions."

3. Emery de Gaal, ed., *Homilies at a First Mass: Joseph Ratzinger's Gift to Priests* (Omaha: IPF Publications, 2016), 19.

4. Gerard McGlone and Len Sperry, *The Inner Life of Priests* (Collegeville, MN: Liturgical Press, 2012), 3.

5. See the writings of John Avila, diocesan priest and doctor of the Church, in *John of Avila: Audi, filia*, trans. Joan Frances Gormley (Mahwah, NJ: Paulist Press, 2006), 219.

6. See Adrian Walker, "Love Alone: Hans Urs von Balthasar as a Master of Theological Renewal," in *Love Alone is Credible*, ed. David Schindler (Grand Rapids, MI: Eerdmans, 2008), 37n42; James Keating, "Falling in Love and Staying in Love: The Gift and Labor of Prayer in Priesthood," *Sacrum Ministerium*, annus XVIII, 1–2 (2012); reprinted in *Seminary Journal* (Spring 2013).

7. Joseph Ratzinger, *On the Way to Jesus Christ* (San Francisco: Ignatius Press, 2005), 40.

8. Walker, "Love Alone."

9. Wilfred Stinissen, *Into Your Hands, Father* (San Francisco: Ignatius Press, 2011), 68.

10. Committee on Priestly Formation of the United States Conference of Catholic Bishops, *Program for Priestly Formation*, 5th ed. (Washington, DC: USCCB, 2006), no. 83.

11. Hans Urs von Balthasar, *The Glory of the Lord: A Theological Aesthetics* (Edinburgh: T&T Clark, 1982), 1:18.

12. Donald Haggerty, *The Contemplative Hunger* (San Francisco: Ignatius Press, 2016), 145.

13. James T. O'Connor, *The Hidden Manna: A Theology of the Eucharist* (San Francisco: Ignatius Press, 2005), 34.

14. Thomas Dubay, *Deep Conversion, Deep Prayer* (San Francisco: Ignatius Press, 2006), 75.

15. Dubay, *Deep Conversion, Deep Prayer*, 77.

16. Lawrence R. Hennessey, "The Spirituality of Priestly Identity: Living Life as a Contemplative Act," *Chicago Studies* 45, no. 2 (Summer 2006).

17. Edith Stein, "The Hidden Life and Epiphany," in *The Hidden Life* (Washington, DC: ICS Publications, 1992), 109–10.

18. Pope Benedict XVI, *Deus Caritas Est* (Rome: Libreria Editrice Vaticana, 2005), no. 7. See http://w2.vatican.va/content/benedict

-xvi/en/encyclicals/documents/hf_ben-xvi_enc_20051225_deus
-caritas-est.html.

19. Joseph Cardinal Ratzinger, *Behold the Pierced One: An Approach to a Spiritual Christology*, trans. G. Harrison (San Francisco: Ignatius Press, 1986), 26.

20. Catherine of Siena, *The Dialogue*, trans. Suzanne Noffke (Mahwah, NJ: Paulist Press, 1980), 120–21.

21. St. Augustine, "Homilies on the First Epistle of John," as quoted in David Meconi, "The Deacon as Symbol of Unifying Loves," *Josephinum Diaconal Review* (Fall 2016): 13.

22. Robert Barron, *Exploring Catholic Theology* (Grand Rapids, MI: Baker, 2015), 142.

3. PRAYER RENEWED

1. "There is no Christian state of life...that does not require self-gift or that is not animated by paschal love. It will, of course, look somewhat different...each called to holiness in a way particular to the demands of their circumstances....But the love in which each participates is none other than Christ's love poured into our hearts by the Holy Spirit. And as different as these [vocations] may be from one another, that love as such is the *viniculum*, the bond that binds the Church together" (Michael Heintz, "Liturgy and Vocation" *Nova et Vetera* 14, no. 4 [Fall 2016]: 1096–97).

2. St. Francis de Sales understood "perfection" not as being "without error," but as the struggle against sin and the choice to stay in relationship with Christ. He counseled that our sins should not disturb us; we should expect them. *God will heal our sins in the relationship*, our worry will not heal them, nor will our self-hate. Perfection is "walking with God," staying in the love relationship, and choosing to no longer isolate oneself from his presence. See *Introduction to the Devout Life* (New York: Random House, 2002) pt. I, V, p. 11; also see Ronald Rolheiser, "Struggling in Prayer," in *Prayer in the Catholic Tradition*, ed. Robert Wicks (Cincinnati: Franciscan Media, 2016), 93ff.

3. Hans Urs von Balthasar, *Engagement with God: The Drama of Christian Discipleship* (San Francisco: Ignatius Press, 2008), 49.

4. Ronald Rolheiser, "Struggling in Prayer," in *Prayer in the Catholic Tradition*, ed. Robert Wicks (Cincinnati: Franciscan Media, 2016), 91.

5. "There is a danger in unrelated desire, anger and reason.... All these must be directed toward God or their isolation leaves one susceptible to adversaries" (Gabriel Bunge, *Despondency: The Spiritual Teaching of Evagrius of Pontus* [Yonkers, NY: St. Vladimir Seminary Press, 2012], 59).

6. John Paul II, *Novo Millennio Ineunte* (Rome: Libreria Editrice Vaticana, 2001), no. 34.

7. Robert Barron, *Exploring Catholic Theology: Essays on God, Liturgy, and Evangelization* (Grand Rapids, MI: Baker Academic, 2015), 183.

8. William Barry, "Spiritual Direction and Prayer," in Wicks, *Prayer in the Catholic Tradition*, 81–82.

9. Robert P. Imbelli, *Rekindling the Christic Imagination: Theological Meditations for the New Evangelization* (Collegeville, MN: Liturgical Press, 2014), 74.

10. Romano Guardini, *The Art of Praying: The Principles and Methods of Christian Prayer* (Manchester, NH: Sophia Institute Press, 1995), 45.

11. "A mentality that can only say, 'That was then, now is now,' is ultimately immature. Knowing and judging past events is the only way to build a meaningful future. Memory is necessary for growth" (Pope Francis, *Amoris Laetitia* 193).

12. John Paul II, *Man and Woman He Created Them: A Theology of the Body* (Boston: Pauline, 2006), 151.

13. St. Augustine, *Confessions*, trans. Henry Chadwick (Oxford: Oxford University Press, 2009), bk. 1, p. 3. "*Cor nostrum inquietum est donec requiescat in Te.*"

14. Benedict XVI, *Deus Caritas Est* (Rome: Libreria Editrice Vaticana, 2005), no. 7.

15. See James Keating, "Seminary Formation and Interior Silence," *Nova et Vetera* 10, no. 2 (Spring 2012).

16. Congregation for the Clergy, "The Gift of the Priestly Vocation" (Vatican City: L'Osservatore Romano, 2016), no. 41.

17. "If we are speaking…to priests about spiritual formation we are speaking about their whole self, not about some part of them, the part other than their body. In modern grammar spiritual has come to mean incorporeal, but in biblical grammar spiritual means belonging to God, being of God. Something becomes spiritual when it becomes obedient to the Father, transparent to the divine Son, a temple for the Holy Spirit, which is why St. Paul says our bodies are temples (1 Corinthians 6:19). Spiritual formation is…to be understood as the formation that the whole [man] undergoes….The internal principle that animates the spiritual life of the priest is pastoral charity, and the 'essential content of pastoral charity is the gift of self in imitation of Christ, and the gift of self is directed toward the Church, particularly that part of it entrusted to him'" (*Pastores Dabo Vobis* 23). See David Fagerberg, "The Ascetical Formation of An Ordained Icon of Love," in *Liturgy and Priestly Formation: Sharing the Life of Christ*, ed. James Keating (Omaha, NE: IPF Publications, 2017). John Paul II also notes, "The priest, who welcomes the call to ministry, is in a position to make this a loving choice, as a result of which the Church and souls become his first interest, and with this concrete spirituality he becomes capable of loving the universal Church and that part of it entrusted to him with the deep love of a husband for his wife. The gift of self has no limits" (*Pastores Dabo Vobis* 23).

18. Angelo Cardinal Scola, *The Nuptial Mystery* (Grand Rapids, MI: Eerdmans, 2005). "It becomes possible for man to transcend the sexual as a function of the species in favor of a form of life in which the agape (nuptiality) of God becomes the full meaning of existence" (80).

19. See Richard Gabuzda, "Relationship, Identity, Mission: A Proposal for Spiritual Formation," in *2005 Symposium: Interiority for Mission: Formation for Priests of the New Evangelization*, ed. Edward Matthews (Omaha, NE: IPF Publications, 2005), 39–51. The current *ratio fundamentalis* on priestly formation from the Congregation for the Clergy implies these same three movements when addressing the discipleship phase (relationship), the configuration phase (identity), and the pastoral phase (mission). See Congregation for the Clergy, "The Gift of the Priestly Vocation" (Vatican City: L'Osservatore Romano, 2016), no. 3.

20. St. Bernard of Clairvaux notes, "This person needs a physician, not a Bridegroom; hence kisses and embraces are not for him, but only oils and ointments, remedies for his wounds." As quoted in Paul

Murray, *In the Grip of Light: The Dark and Bright Journey of Christian Contemplation* (London: Bloomsbury Continuum, 2012), 67.

4. MINISTRY

1. Sally Read, *Night's Bright Darkness: A Modern Conversion Story* (San Francisco: Ignatius Press, 2016), 61–62.

2. Benedict XVI, "Meeting with the Clergy," Warsaw Cathedral, Poland, May 25, 2006; author's emphasis.

3. Congregation for the Clergy, "The Gift of the Priestly Vocation," no. 97.

4. Benedict XVI, *A School of Prayer: The Saints Show Us How to Pray* (San Francisco: Ignatius Press, 2012), 150.

5. It is only the deacon, and deacon become priest, who can stand in the ambo proclaiming salvation as it is being offered in the Eucharist. There is, of course, much conversation around the "power" that is gifted to a deacon upon ordination. Is it really a *unique power* or simply a virtue unleashed at ordination strengthening him to be sent to proclaim and serve? I believe that the unique role of diaconal proclamation of the Gospel *during the Liturgy of the Eucharist* is this office's defining sacramental power. Obviously, that has yet to be agreed upon by theologians and is not taught by the Magisterium as definitive. For further reading on this subject, see USCCB, *Compendium on the Diaconate* (Washington, DC: USCCB, 2015) 345–61; also see David Lopez, "Order of Levitical Blessing: Fruitfully Reclaiming a Patristic, Liturgical Typology of the Diaconate," *Antiphon* 19 (2015): 52–78.

6. Peter Williamson, "Preparing Seminarians for the Ministry of the Word in Light of *Verbum Domini*," in *Verbum Domini and the Complementarity of Exegesis and Theology*, ed. Scott Carl (Grand Rapids, MI: Eerdmans, 2015), 88.

7. Jean Corbon, *The Wellspring of Worship* (San Francisco: Ignatius Press, 2005), 37.

8. André Guitton, *Peter Julian Eymard: Apostle of the Eucharist* (Ponteranica, Italy: Centro Eucharistico, 1996), 36, 258–59.

9. Jorge Carlos Patrón Wong, "Foundations of Priestly Formation," accessed March 24, 2017, http://www.clerus.va/content/clerus/en/notizie/new4.html. Author's emphasis.

10. Han Urs von Balthasar, *Mysterium Paschale* (Grand Rapids, MI: Eerdmans, 1990), 131.

11. Thomas J. Lane, *The Catholic Priesthood: Biblical Foundations* (Steubenville, OH: Emmaus Road Publishing, 2016), 111.

12. Matthew Levering, *Christ and the Catholic Priesthood: Ecclesial Hierarchy and the Pattern of the Trinity* (Mundelein, IL: Hillenbrand Books, 2010), 93.

13. Benedict XVI, *Verbum Domini* (Rome: Libreria Editrice Vaticana, 2010), no. 15.

14. Angelo Scola, *Hans Urs von Balthasar: A Theological Style* (Grand Rapids, MI: Eerdmans, 1995), 87, wherein he posits the *thirst of reason* is the unbeknownst drive to find rest *in the truth who is God* and not in the idols of each succeeding culture.

15. Benedict XVI, *Verbum Domini*, no. 11, author's emphasis.

16. Pope Francis, *Evangelii Gaudium* (Rome: Libreria Editrice Vaticana, 2013), nos. 172–73.

17. Joseph Ratzinger, *God and the World: A Conversation with Peter Seewald* (San Francisco: Ignatius Press, 2002), 190.

18. Iain Matthew, *The Impact of God: Soundings from St John of the Cross* (London: Hodder & Stoughton, 1995), 56–57.

19. Bl. Columba Marmion, *Christ the Life of the Soul* (Tacoma, WA: Angelico Press, 2012), 186.

20. Jacques Philippe, *Time for God* (New York: Scepter Publishers, 2008), 56.

21. Joseph Cardinal Ratzinger, *Introduction to Christianity* (San Francisco: Ignatius Press, 2004), 289.

22. Benedict XVI, *Deus Caritas Est* (Rome: Libreria Editrice Vaticana, 2005), nos. 5, 7. Author's emphasis.

23. Hans Urs von Balthasar, *Mysterium Paschale* (Grand Rapids, MI: Eerdmans, 1990), 131.

5. UNITED IN HOLY ORDERS

1. Pope Emeritus Benedict XVI, *Called to Holiness: On Love, Vocation, and Formation* (Washington, DC: CUA Press, 2017), 218.

2. The best contemporary meditation on priestly celibacy is found in Gary B. Selin, *Priestly Celibacy: Theological Foundations* (Washington, DC: CUA Press, 2016).

3. I discuss the gift of celibacy for deacons elsewhere; here, I am focusing only on the married deacon. See James Keating, *The Heart of the Diaconate: Communion with the Servant Mysteries of Christ* (Mahwah, NJ: Paulist Press, 2016), 28–33.

4. John Paul II, *Pastores Dabo Vobis* (Rome: Libreria Editrice Vaticana, 1992), 29.

5. Thomas J. Lane, *The Catholic Priesthood: Biblical Foundations* (Steubenville, OH: Emmaus Road Publishing, 2016), 178.

6. Benedict XVI, "Meeting with the Clergy," Warsaw Cathedral, Poland, May 25, 2006.